☐ Holdings
Genre _____
Genre _____
☑ RFID
☑ Final check

DISCARDED

D0786986

MODERN WORLD NATIONS

Austria

Alan Allport

Series Consulting Editor
Charles F. Gritzner
South Dakota State University

Lincoln Public Library

3 7496 00134807 4

CHELSEA HOUSE
P U B L I S H E R S
An imprint of Infobase Publishing

Frontispiece: Flag of Austria

Cover: Farmland with conical haystacks surrounding the village of St. Georgen in the Lieser River Valley, Carinthia, Austria.

Austria

Copyright © 2002 by Infobase Publishing

All rights reserved. No part of this book may be reproduced or utilized in any form or by any means, electronic or mechanical, including photocopying, recording, or by any information storage or retrieval systems, without permission in writing from the publisher. For information contact:

Chelsea House
An imprint of Infobase Publishing
132 West 31st Street
New York NY 10001

Library of Congress Cataloging-in-Publication Data

Allport, Alan, 1970–
  Austria / by Allan Allport.
    p. cm. — (Modern world nations)
Includes bibliographical references and index.
  ISBN 0-7910-6775-0
1. Austria—History—Juvenile literature. 2. Austria—Social life and customs—Juvenile literature. I. Title. II. Series.
DB17 .A293 2002
  943.6—dc21   2002003711

Chelsea House books are available at special discounts when purchased in bulk quantities for businesses, associations, institutions, or sales promotions. Please call our Special Sales Department in New York at (212) 967-8800 or (800) 322-8755.

You can find Chelsea House on the World Wide Web at http://www.chelseahouse.com

Text and cover design by Takeshi Takahashi

Printed in the United States of America

Bang 21C 10 9 8 7 6 5 4 3 2

This book is printed on acid-free paper.

Table of Contents

Austria

Austria has long been renowned for its beautiful Alpine scenery, but few know that this country's history spans more than a thousand years. Something of Austria's rich architectural and religious traditions can be seen in this view of the 12th century Klosterneuburg Abbey on the Danube River.

Introduction

An American asked to describe something stereotypically Austrian might come up with a tourist's montage of picturesque lakes and mountains, baroque churches, coffeehouses, and Mozart operas. Perhaps the American would also mention *The Sound of Music,* the Rodgers and Hammerstein stage musical that was turned into a hugely successful 1965 movie starring Julie Andrews and Christopher Plummer. Generations of musical fans have grown up knowing and loving *The Sound of Music,* itself an adaptation of the real-life story of the von Trapp family. And, next to Mozart, the von Trapp family—or at least the film version of their lives—is perhaps Austria's greatest cultural export.

However, a moviegoer who saw *The Sound of Music* without knowing anything else about Austria might be a bit perplexed by some of the story's details. How, for instance, did Captain Georg

During World War I, Baron Georg von Trapp served the Austro-Hungarian Empire as a submarine commander. More than twenty years later, in the face of Nazi invasion, von Trapp led his family out of Austria and into exile – a decision only recently honored by the Austrian government.

von Trapp become a naval officer in the first place since Austria is a landlocked country with no coasts or ports? Why did the Austrians allow the Nazis to take over their country—and why is it that some of them welcomed the conquest, while others, like the von Trapps, opposed it so much that they fled abroad to safety?

The answer to the first question is that some 20 years before the story is set, Austria had been part of a much larger

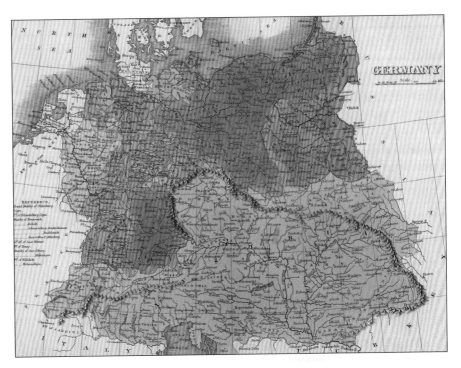

As this 1826 map of Germany shows, Austria (in pink) once stretched far beyond her present-day boundaries. Her borders largely defined by mountains to the north, Austria reached south into what is now Italy, giving her valuable access to the rich trade of the Mediterranean Sea.

empire that included the port city of Trieste, now in Italy, and much of the Dalmatian coast in what is now Croatia. Captain von Trapp was in his youth an officer in this imperial navy—although the movie doesn't mention this, he was in real-life an intrepid submarine commander who had had many daring adventures during World War I. At the end of the war, the Austro-Hungarian Empire was divided up, and Austria lost its navy along with its coastline.

The answer to the second question is that Austria at the time of *The Sound of Music* was in political turmoil, with the government effectively a dictatorship, and many Austrians had lost confidence in their leaders—indeed, they no longer believed that Austria should exist at all and that it should again

While Austria was much larger in the 19th century, today it is roughly the size of the state of Maine and is surrounded by a number of nations. At the end of World War I, the Austro-Hungarian Empire was divided up, and Austria lost its coastline.

be part of a much larger empire, this time the Third Reich of Adolf Hitler (who was himself born in Austria). Other Austrians were appalled at the collapse of democracy in their country, and tens of thousands of them followed the von

Trapps into exile abroad. Some even did as Maria, the Captain, and their children did and emigrated to the United States.

Austria, it turns out, has a very complicated and turbulent as well as fascinating history and culture, and this book is a very short introduction to Austrians and their land, past and present. It talks about the geography of Austria and the way this has shaped the development and traditions of its people; their social structure, attitudes and beliefs; the country's economy and political system; and the enormous contribution Austria has made to the world's arts and culture. Austria is by American standards a fairly small place, with a population only about the size of North Carolina's and a landmass no bigger than Maine's. But individual Austrians have had a huge influence on history, both good and bad, and at one time Austria was one of the political superpowers of the world; one of its rulers even claimed sovereignty over almost the entire western hemisphere.

Austria today does not play such a commanding role on the international scene. But it is nonetheless a country of great beauty and heritage that lies geographically and symbolically at the heart of Europe, and the story of its often-difficult progress toward prosperity and democracy provides both a model and a warning for the present day.

Snow-covered Mount Grossglockner is Austria's highest peak, a part of the Alpine chain that stands over 12,000 feet above sea level. Surprisingly, however, other areas of the country, those bordering the eastern Great Hungarian Plain, are relatively flat.

CHAPTER

2

The Land

"The Austrian has a fatherland, and rightly loves it," wrote the 18th-century German playwright Friedrich Schiller. As we will see in the following chapters, Austrians have not always agreed about what the nature of that "fatherland" is. But Austria as a place is undoubtedly easy to love. It has one of the most spectacular landscapes in the world, and its enormous modern-day tourist industry is testament to the appeal of the country's natural, as well as its man-made, environment. The very beauty of Austrian topography has ironically been more of a challenge than a boon to its history, however. Though ideal for picture postcards, Austria's daunting terrain is much less suited to settlement and agriculture and has constricted the country's demographic development. Austrians, like all peoples, have to some extent shaped their economic, social, and cultural ideas to reflect the circumstances of the geography that surrounds them. One outcome of this has been a strong local identification with the varied regions from which Austrians come.

A Landscape of Beauty

Austria is a medium-sized European country in the southern-central part of the continent, surrounded by several other nations: Switzerland and the tiny duchy of Liechtenstein to the west, Germany to the northwest, the Czech Republic to the north, Slovakia to the northeast, Hungary to the east, and Slovenia and Italy to the south. At 32,378 square miles (83,859 square kilometers), Austria is roughly the size of Maine. It is a somewhat pear-shaped land, with a long, thin western end that bulges out as one travels farther eastward. The distance from west to east is approximately 340 miles (547 kilometers)—about the driving distance from New York City to Richmond, Virginia. Austria is subdivided into nine self-governing "Länder," or federal provinces: Burgenland, Carinthia, Lower Austria, Upper Austria, Salzburg, Styria, Tyrol, Vienna, and Vorarlberg.

The single most dominant feature of the country's landscape is its mountains. Austria is part of the great European Alpine chain, and almost two-thirds of the country is classed as mountainous. There are no huge individual peaks in Austria; the highest mountain—Grossglockner—measures in at a relatively modest 12,460 feet (3,798 meters). But there are fairly large areas of the Austrian Alps that rise above 10,000 feet (3,048 meters), and these suffer correspondingly severe weather and temperature conditions throughout the year. The most mountainous part of the country is to the west and south, and as one heads eastward, the Alps gently recede into foothills that eventually flatten out to become part of the Great Hungarian Plain at the eastern border. Despite Austria's reputation as a land of hills, some eastern parts of the country are very flat indeed—so much so

The country map of Austria shows that its most dominant feature is its mountains, which are part of the European Alpine chain. Large areas of the Austrian Alps rise above 10,000 feet (3,048 meters) and have severe weather and temperature conditions throughout the year.

that flash floods are a serious environmental hazard during the oftentimes-stormy summer months. But it nonetheless true that for most people, both inside and outside the country, the Alps are the definitive symbol of the Austrian national landscape.

Three other natural features define much of Austrian geography. The first is the country's green blanket of forest. Even after more than a century of heavy industrialization, about two-fifths of Austria is still covered with woodland, making it the most densely forested country in central Europe, with thick belts of spruce, beech, oak, and conifers. This dense foliage provides a home to a plethora of woodland animals straight out of fairytale lore, including wolves, bears, wild boar, deer, and birds of prey. Rich hunting opportunities encouraged generations of aristocratic sportsmen to take their summer vacations at family hunting lodges deep in the Austrian forests.

Another characteristic part of the Austrian countryside is its many lakes. These predominate in mountain and subalpine regions, particularly the beautiful Salzkammergut, a hilly central district of limestone massifs punctuated by water. The two largest lakes in Austria are at opposite ends of the country and represent the geographical extremes of its territory; Lake Constance forms a dramatic rift in the westernmost mountains of Vorarlberg, while the marshlike, salty Neusiedler See in the east is extremely shallow—only 4 to 6 feet (1.2 to 1.8 meters) deep at most—and almost disappears during hot summers.

The last significant feature of Austrian geography, and the only serious competitor with the Alps as the defining icon of the country's natural heritage, is the Danube. One of the great river systems of the world, coursing for 1,770 miles (2,849 kilometers) from the Black Forest in western Germany to the Black Sea, the Danube, in addition to providing the inspiration for some of Austria's most enduring artistic works, gives the northeast corner of Austria—through which it flows for 220 miles (350 kilometers)—a vital commercial and agricultural base. Always one of Austria's lifelines to the outside world, the Danube's usefulness as a channel of trade has been increased even more by the opening in 1992 of a canal linking it to the Rhine and the Main, allowing river traffic to travel directly from the North Sea to the Black Sea and beyond. Indeed, the Danube is so critical to the countries that border it that its pollution has become a serious international controversy in recent years.

Austria's climate is an eccentric one, reflecting its central position on the European mainland. The Austrian Alps are a meeting point for weather patterns originally emanating from the North Atlantic, the Mediterranean, and the

Another outstanding feature of Austria's geography is the Danube River, which stretches over 1,700 miles from Germany to the Black Sea. In this stunning view, we see the ruins of an ancient castle, perched high above the river valley.

Ukrainian steppe, and the combination of these can produce unstable and occasionally bizarre quirks of temperature and precipitation. Although the country below the mountainous snow zone is generally temperate, eastern Austria in the summer is often alternately basted with hot dry winds from southern Russia and lashed by violent rainstorms. Farther west, the Salzburg region is home to the peculiar phenomenon known as *Schnürlregen,* a type of rain that comes down not in drops but in continuous ribbonlike streams. And moody Austrians, especially in the Tyrol, have always blamed their state of mind on the so-called *Föhn,* a warm and moist air mass from the south that it is sometimes claimed induces depression and even suicide. But despite these idiosyncratic touches, Austria has a reasonably consistent seasonal cycle that does not place great handicaps in the way of farmers.

However, what do create handicaps for farmers—or, for that matter, any kind of dense population growth—are the selfsame geographical features that combine to make Austria a place of unsurpassed beauty: the poor and uneven quality of the land caused by the mountainous terrain and the interspersed woods and lakes. Less than one-fifth of Austria's soil is really suitable for conventional agriculture. Much of the grassland is at a high altitude, which is used as pasture for dairy cattle during the summer months but is not appropriate for growing cereal crops or animal fodder. The best farming land is predominantly to the north and east, in Upper and Lower Austria, Burgenland, and parts of Styria, and not surprisingly these areas have been the focus of human settlement throughout most of Austria's history. The scarcity of useful food-producing land, plus its geographical imbalance, is reflected in the fact that Austria has a very low population density compared to other rich European countries—closer to that of the Balkans than the industrialized West—and the majority of Austrians (over two-thirds) live in the more sustainable Danubian region beyond the Alps. In the mountainous western region the population is mostly restricted to small river valleys, which until recent advances in communication were largely cut off from one another. Nearly all Austrians live in just two-fifths of the country's territory; the remaining area supports a very low and widely scattered population.

But despite these formidable natural obstacles Austria has historically been a major conduit for people, goods and information, a European crossroads that connects west to east and north to south. The narrow 4,511-foot-high (1,375 meters) Brenner Pass is the most important land link between southern Germany and Italy's Po River Valley, a route for invading armies used by the Romans onward and a channel of trade from the Mediterranean to the Baltic and North Seas since late medieval times. And as we have already noted, the River Danube is the principal commercial artery between western and southeastern Europe. The river's strategic significance is highlighted by the string of castles and fortifications that bedeck its banks, and Austria's control of a couple of hundred of those miles has long afforded it a military and political significance that has not always been in its best interest. Turkish ambitions in Europe from the 15th century on, for example, depended on a secure line of communications back to their imperial capital at Constantinople (modern-day Istanbul), and this meant advancing along the Danube; for hundreds of years Austria had to act as Europe's frontier guard against the onslaught of the Ottoman invaders. There has also been a corresponding traffic of people from west to east, with merchants, pilgrims, and crusaders journeying to the cities and shrines of the Near East and the Holy Land. Nowadays the old pilgrim routes have been supplanted by a dense inter-state (*Autobahn*) road network that acts as a transportation hub for European commerce.

Austria can be subdivided into three major geographical regions: the western Alpine region of Vorarlberg, Tyrol, Salzburg and Carinthia; the central foothill region of Styria and Upper Austria; and the eastern predominantly flatter plains region of Lower Austria and Burgenland. It is important to keep in mind that these subdivisions are somewhat arbitrary—all of Austria's provinces contain some hills and mountains, for example—but however imperfectly, they do represent a real shift in the topographical character of the country.

The Alpine West

The Austrian Alps consist of three major groups, northern, central, and southern. The northern and southern mountain chains are limestone, while the central peaks are made up of softer crystalline rocks. Glaciers have cut dramatic clefts in the mountain faces and formed lush valleys in which the majority of settlements are clustered. The isolated circumstances of this life have been reflected in a rugged individualist ethos within the local communities, which have a long history of political independence from Vienna.

Vorarlberg is the smallest (excepting the capital itself) and most westerly of all Austria's provinces, and before the construction of the Arlberg tunnel in 1978, it was effectively cut off from the rest of the country during winter. Despite its rustic nature and inhospitable terrain, it is one of the most heavily industrialized regions of Austria and has an ancient textile and dairy-farming industry; its largest city, Dornbirn, is an important manufacturing center. Culturally close to their Swiss neighbors, the citizens of Vorarlberg attempted to secede to Switzerland after the breakup of the Habsburg Empire. The locals have now accommodated themselves to life as Austrians, perhaps encouraged by the fact that they possess the highest income per head in the country.

Tyrol lies at the heart of the Austrian Alps, and one of its more dubious claims is that it has the lowest percentage of useable arable land (3 percent) of any national province; barely 15 percent of Tyrol is permanently settled. Boasting daunting mountain peaks, its capital, Innsbruck, is a major winter-sports destination and has hosted two Winter Olympics, which has helped to give Tyrol the highest earnings from tourism of all Austria's provinces. The medieval silver mines that once enriched the local nobility were exhausted by the 17th century, and aside from tourism the region's most significant economic activity is cattle and dairy farming. Tyrolean patriots are famous for waging an effective guerilla war against Napoleon Bonaparte in the early 1800s, but the province was less fortunate a century later when it was carved in two by the Treaty of St. Germain, which awarded South Tyrol to Italy.

Salzburg, a province that shares its name with its principal city, was an independent bishopric outside of Austria until 1816. The city built its gorgeous Baroque churches with the taxes acquired from mining deposits of gold, silver, and salt—for which the region is named—deposits, and salt production is still an important factor in the local economy; but nowadays Salzburgers prefer to mine the rich reputation of their most famous son, Wolfgang Amadeus Mozart. Salzburg also includes the Krimml Falls, the largest waterfalls in Europe.

Carinthia is the southernmost of Austria's provinces, and its position south of the major Alpine groups means that it enjoys a warmer, more consistent summer temperature than the rest of the country. Carinthia is home to over 2,000 lakes, including four very large bodies of water, and the Riviera-like climate has particular appeal for tourists from elsewhere in Austria. Carinthia's timber industry is especially important for the regional economy. The province borders Slovenia, formerly part of Yugoslavia, and has a small Slovenian ethnic minority. Parts of Carinthia were claimed by the Yugoslavs after both World Wars, and there were violent clashes across the frontier.

Perhaps best known as the birthplace of composer Wolfgang Amadeus Mozart, Salzburg is a culturally rich city that built its fortunes from rich mining deposits in the area. Overlooked by dramatic mountains and an eleventh-century fortress, the city is home to some of the region's most beautiful churches.

The Central Foothills

The most notable feature of this region is the Salzkammergut, an area of forested crags and lakes that has a good claim to be the loveliest of all Austria's scenic landscapes and has enjoyed a flourishing tourist industry since at least the 19th century. More suitable for agriculture and with less treacherous communications than the west, central Austria is consequently more populous and has a high industrial concentration in its large cities.

Styria ("Steiermark" in German) is known as the Green Province because of its thick forests, which cover over half the countryside. Woodland is interspersed with pastures and vineyards that produce part of Austria's growing wine export trade. Heavy mining operations take place in Styria, which includes the well-known Erzberg, or Iron Mountain; the largest provincial city, Graz—Austria's second city after Vienna and long its political and cultural rival—is also heavily industrialized. The decline in world demand for heavy industrial goods depressed the local economy in the last few decades, but a switch to service industries has aided recovery—as have the frequent visits of Graz's celebrated son Arnold Schwarzenegger.

Upper Austria makes up one-quarter of the country's industrial output, and though the province's major city, Linz, is smaller than Graz, Linz's position on the Danube gives it particular commercial importance. Upper Austria is also a center of agriculture, and there are significant oil and natural-gas fields located there. Like all of Austria's provinces, it contains some magnificent scenery, with granite hills surrounded by meadows and woods. There are several well-preserved medieval towns, including Braunau, which has the uncomfortable distinction of being Adolf Hitler's childhood home.

The Eastern Plains

Although "plains" is something of a misnomer because Lower Austria and Burgenland contain their share of high ground as well, the provinces at the eastward extreme of Austria are the flattest in the country and correspondingly among the most hospitable to human settlement.

Lower Austria surrounds the city of Vienna, which administratively is a federal province in its own right, though the two obviously share a common historical and geographical heritage. Lower Austria is the largest of the nine provinces and the Austrian political heartland—the original source of the name "Austria" and the basis of the Eastern March, from which the country derives its origins. As well as its important farming base, the area is also Austria's biggest wine producer. The so-called Vienna Woods—an area of gently rolling hillsides, small farms, and forests close to the metropolis—mark the division between city and countryside.

Vienna itself has sometimes been described as a capital without an empire, a great city that became one of the artistic centers of European culture in its 19th-century heyday and that now sits rather awkwardly within a small and parochial country. With one-fifth of all Austrians being Viennese, the city naturally plays a key role in the life of the nation—a role that is sometimes resented by those in the far-flung provinces.

Burgenland has a natural and man-made heritage quite unlike any other region of Austria. Until the creation of the First Republic, Burgenland was part of Hungary; geographically it is the westernmost extreme of the Puszta, or Great Hungarian Plain, and so is closer in landscape to eastern than central Europe. Market gardening of fruit and vegetables is an important local industry, as is the area's distinctive wine from its vineyards. The Hungarian flavor is maintained by such local tourist attractions as the huge and opulent Esterházy Palace, home of one of Hungary's great aristocratic families, and the one-time workplace of the composer Franz Joseph Haydn.

Ecological Issues

Throughout this chapter we have seen that two factors, above all, have influenced Austria's development: its marginal land resources and its centrality in Europe's transport and communications system. In recent years the combination of these two has given rise to serious environmental problems, for the huge increases in Europe's economic activity—especially since the end of the Cold War and the rebuilding of the former Eastern Bloc—have put great stress on the inherently fragile Austrian ecosystem. Austrians have responded to this threat with strong political pressure for "green"—i.e., environmentally friendly—policies.

About one-quarter of all the traffic using Austria's Autobahn system is made up of large commercial trucks hauling goods across the Continent. The routes they take wind through the mountainous western provinces—areas that are particularly vulnerable to environmental damage from noise and exhaust pollution. The trans-European weather patterns that meet in the Austrian Alps also import polluted air from northwest Europe, Italy, and the former communist countries of Eastern Europe; the latter source is especially worrisome for Austrians because many of these countries have lax or nonexistent pollution-control laws. By the early 1990s it was estimated that about four-tenths of Austria's vast forests had been damaged by acid rain generated from the country's own industrial plants as well as that which comes in from abroad. Depletion of woodland in mountain areas has caused other environmental hazards; as the treeline that naturally soaks up snow and rain disappears, Alpine provinces have suffered greater incidences of mudslides, flash floods, and avalanches. Austria's success at attracting tourists has proved a mixed blessing, for the huge numbers of incoming visitors during the vacation season have overloaded the modest infrastructures of the remote western provinces.

Aiming to counter these threats to their delicate ecological balance, Austria's government and people have tried to introduce domestic legislation reducing environmental damage as well as negotiate international agreements to limit problems emanating from abroad. Vienna is engaged in discussions with the European Union (EU) to restrict the amount of commercial traffic that can enter the country at any one time and encourage the greater use of railroads for goods transit. Similar initiatives to clean up fossil-fuel power stations, one of the principal sources of acid rain, are under way. Austrians are fastidious about recycling, and the country is the third largest recycler of paper in the world. Advertising campaigns to propagate the idea of so-called green tourism, which has a less destructive effect on the natural environment, have begun. Austria was also the first country in Europe to formally ban—by popular referendum—the use of atomic energy within its own borders, although critics have pointed out that the country turns a blind eye to importing nuclear-generated power from neighboring sources. A small but growing parliamentary Green Party now pushes for more stringent environmental legislation in Vienna.

It can be seen from all this that Austria's environmental problems are, above all, international problems, and that they can only be effectively tackled by cooperation from all the countries of the region. The fate of the River Danube is perhaps the best example of this. Nine countries share the Danube, and all of them exploit its transport, hydroelectric, fishing, irrigation, and water-supply potential. As use of the river has increased—particularly in the developing east—its resources have correspondingly suffered; the Danube's waters are no longer safely drinkable because of the industrial toxicants pumped into it from chemical and manufacturing plants, its fishing grounds have been depleted, and the addition of new canals and dams has influenced the river's course and flow in a perilously unpredictable way. No single country can legislate a cleanup of the Danube in isolation because all the members of the Danubian community are equally responsible for its preservation.

Issues like the Danube's pollution have played an important role in Austria's sometimes-fractured relationship with the European Union. Critics of EU expansion insist that the Union must not allow former Eastern Bloc countries to become members unless they provide adequate environmental safeguards for their industry. EU supporters have suggested that it's only the support and discipline of the Union that will encourage the East to do this in the first place.

Habsburg ruler, Franz Joseph (1830-1916) guided Austria out of an era of revolutionary turmoil she suffered during the mid-1800s. To answer pressure from his Hungarian subjects, Franz Joseph issued the Compromise of 1867, creating what would be known as the Austro-Hungarian Empire.

3

The Early History of Austria

Historically, what is Austria? This is not a straightforward question. Nowadays Austria is defined as the landlocked, partly mountainous, heavily forested country in south-central Europe that we described in Chapter 2. But before 1918, when this modern republic was created, "Austria" was a gigantic multinational, multilingual empire stretching from southern Galicia in modern Poland to the Adriatic shore and from the Carpathian Mountains in Romania to the borders of Switzerland. These were the lands of the Habsburgs, probably the most extraordinary family in European history. The Austria we know today was just another corner of a much larger political unit—and in many respects not even a very important corner.

Modern Austrians speak of their history in two separate ways to reflect this dual identity: There is the history of Austria as it is defined nowadays, and then there is the *Kaiserzeit,* the history of all the lands of the Habsburgs. By necessity, this chapter will jump between the two—sometimes discussing events within the borders of the modern Republic and sometimes events that took place in what are now Hungary, Poland, the Czech Republic, and so on.

Austria Before the Habsburgs

Evidence of humans settling in Austria goes back at least 7,000 years, although little is known about these first inhabitants, and the first Austrians may have appeared even earlier. The story becomes a little clearer by the Early Iron Age, around 1000–400 B.C., when the so-called Hallstatt civilization, named after the archeological site where it was first discovered, was active. The Hallstatt people were the first to exploit the region's salt deposits and develop a primitive mining industry as well as leave behind a material legacy in the form of pottery, brooches, weaponry, and a formalized artistic style based on bird motifs.

From about 400 B.C. onward, Celtic tribes occupied the area and founded the kingdom of Noricum, Austria's first recognizable political unit. But the strategic value of the Danube as well as the region's iron resources were not lost on another ambitious people, the Romans. After a couple of centuries of tentative probing, the legions marched north, overwhelmed Noricum, and established an imperial presence along the line of the river, briefly integrating Austria into the culture of the ancient Mediterranean and Near East. Vienna—called Vindobona by the Romans— became a significant military and administrative center at this time, and Christianity trickled into Austria along with colonists from the south.

Roman suzerainty over Austria was fairly short-lived, however, as by 166–180 A.D. Germanic tribes were already plundering the newly established provinces, and despite initially repelling these invaders, the Roman emperors found it increasingly difficult—and unprofitable—to maintain control of their distant and not very prosperous Danubian frontier. By the 5th century A.D. the Romans had essentially given up, and for several hundred years afterward the region was contested by successive waves of barbarian tribes, culminating in a showdown between the Slavic Avars and the Germanic Bavarians.

The latter had a powerful patron in the form of the Frankish ruler Charlemagne (reigning 771–814), whose empire stretched across much of northwestern Europe. This tipped the scales in favor of the Bavarians, who turned Austria into a fortified border "march," or frontier, of the Frankish empire, known as the Eastern March. The distinctive character of the Austrian Germanic dialect is an inheritance from these Bavarian settlers.

The seesaw battle was not over yet, however, as in 880 A.D. the Eastern March was conquered by new interlopers, this time Magyars from what is today Hungary. It was not until 955 that a descendent of Charlemagne, King Otto I (reigning 936–976), smashed the nomadic Magyars at the battle of the Lechfeld and returned Austria to the Frankish-German fold, this time for good.

In 976 A.D. the German emperor installed Leopold I of the House of Babenberg (reigning 976–994) as ruler of Austria. The Babenbergs were to hold this position for the next 300 years, and their reign saw the consolidation of many of Austria's most characteristic features. The word "Austria" itself—*Österreich* in German, literally translating as "eastern realm"—was used to describe the region for the first time. (In 1996 modern Austrians celebrated the thousandth anniversary of this naming). Austria received the status of a duchy and began to exhibit more practical independence from the German crown. By the late 1100s the ducal capital had moved to Vienna, henceforth the

This shows medieval Vienna as it appeared in a woodcut print illustration from an historical volume of the time.

political center of the country. A canon of local common law emerged. The red-white-red color scheme that today makes up the Austrian flag was invented. The Babenbergs fostered a rich cultural life at their courts; "Nibelunglied"

("Song of the Nibelung") one of the German language's most influential poems, was written under their auspices. Monasteries, towns, and roads were built. All of this cost money, and one Babenberg, Leopold V (reigning 1177–1194), dreamed up an enterprising means of funding his development plans when he kidnapped King Richard "the Lionheart," who was returning to England from the Crusades in the Holy Land via Austria, and held him to ransom.

Like most of the princes of Germany at the time the Babenbergs found themselves embroiled in various political conflicts, including the continuous squabbling between the nobility and the church, which had considerable secular as well as spiritual authority in the Middle Ages. The resulting wars and alliances caused a bewildering series of divisions and absorptions of Austrian territory, particularly as the Babenbergs practiced the traditional partition of land between the inheriting sons of the ruler. But the long-term trend was for the duchy's borders to expand, from the region immediately adjoining the River Danube southward toward what is now the province of Styria. Although there was much territorial jockeying to come, the distinctive outline of an Austrian nation was starting to emerge.

However, the Babenbergs would not survive to see the fruition of their work. After Duke Frederick II (reigning 1230–1246) died leaving no male heir, the claim to the duchy was contested. This allowed Otakar II, prince of nearby Bohemia (reigning 1253–1278), to finagle his way into the Viennese inheritance. Otakar proved a bit too successful for his own good because his expansion frightened the other German nobles so much that they leagued together to expel him from Austria; in 1278 at the battle of the Marchfeld, Otaker was defeated and killed by an army led by Count Rudolf I of Habsburg (1218–1291), the head of the family that would dominate Austrian history for the next 700 years.

Enter The Habsburgs

The reason that Count Rudolf led the coalition against Otakar was that five years earlier he had been elected emperor of the Holy Roman Empire by his fellow German princes. The Holy Roman Empire was the legacy of Charlemagne, the Frankish emperor who had sponsored the creation of the first Austrian frontier. Charlemagne's original empire had extended across modern France, the Low Countries, Germany, and northern Italy, but by Rudolf's time it had become for most practical purposes an all-German affair. At first the Habsburg rulers were only elected as Holy Roman Emperor every now and again. But after 1440 they monopolized the office, and it became in effect a hereditary Austrian title until the empire's dissolution in 1806. For centuries ruling over Austria came bundled with the extra opportunities and headaches of also being Holy Roman Emperor.

The early Habsburgs introduced new Austrian institutions. They founded the University of Vienna in 1365 and built a magnificent gothic cathedral, St. Stephen's, in the city center. This triumph of medieval architecture dominates the Viennese skyline even today, and within its catacombs are the preserved entrails of the Habsburg rulers, housed in individual bronze caskets. (Other Habsburg body parts can be found elsewhere in the city—their hearts are in the nearby Augustinian church, and the rest of their mortal remains are encased in monumental sarcophagi in the Capuchin Crypt.)

One of the most colorful of the early Habsburg monarchs was Frederick III (reigning 1440–1493). Amongst Frederick's contributions to the family inheritance was an ingenious forgery, the "Privilegium Maius," which claimed all sorts of extravagant and spurious rights for Austria within the Holy Roman Empire. Frederick had a mysterious motto, a.e.i.o.u., which he was fond of having doodled in the

Early Habsburg ruler Frederick III, who reigned from 1440-1493, did much to extend Austria's land holdings and influence. This sixteenth-century fresco shows the marriage of Frederick to Eleonora of Portugal.

archways and portals of his castles and public buildings. This cryptic message has inspired speculation throughout history; it is probably an acronym in Latin and old German for "Austria's destiny is to rule over the whole world."

Frederick may have had his whimsical diversions, but when it came to the business of expanding the Habsburg lands, he was deadly serious. His master plan for this involved not conquest but a far more potent weapon in the medieval era: the wedding ring. Carefully selected marriages could allow an ambitious family to make major territorial gains through inheritance, and the Habsburgs were acknowledged masters of the craft—as the saying went: "Let others wage war; you, happy Austria, marry!" A series of fortuitous births and deaths meant that by the early 1500s, a single Habsburg prince, Charles V (1500–1558), ruled Austria, Burgundy (in eastern France), the Netherlands, Spain—at the time the richest and most powerful country in Europe— southern Italy, and the new lands of the Americas, discovered by Europeans just two decades earlier courtesy of Christopher Columbus. This was more than just a valuable inheritance; it was the creation of a world empire.

In practice, however, the Habsburg lands were less cohesive than they seemed. It quickly became clear that the government infrastructure of the day was too primitive to allow one man to control such a huge and scattered empire. Charles therefore deputized his younger brother Ferdinand (1503–1564) to rule Austria in his place while he concentrated his attentions on Spain. This arrangement was soon codified into law, and it was also agreed that Ferdinand would become Holy Roman Emperor after Charles. The Habsburg dynasty split into two branches, with Charles's descendents forming the so-called Spanish Habsburgs and Ferdinand's children continuing the Austrian Habsburgs. Although the branches would remain closely associated until 1700, when the Spanish Habsburg line died out, they conducted their future business independently of one another.

Europe was at the same time being shaken by the religious movement known as the Protestant Reformation, which had started in 1517 when Martin Luther, a German priest in the town of Wittenberg, presented his congregation with a series of complaints against ecclesiastical practices. Something about the passionate intensity of Luther's protest and the defiance with which he faced Papal demands to repent ignited a latent powderkeg of rebellion within Europe—and particularly within the Holy Roman Empire. By the 1520s the continent was abuzz with heretical ideas, and Luther's supporters—who became known as "Protestants"—had attracted the patronage of some of the German princes. Austria was quickly affected by this turmoil. News about the Protestant challenge to Rome began to reach Austria from the northern German universities, spread in part by the new technology of printing, and converts accumulated at an astonishing rate. It has been estimated that by the time of Luther's death in 1546, around 90 percent of the Austrian population had turned Protestant.

As staunch defenders of the Catholic faith, both Charles V and Ferdinand strove to suppress the Protestant heresy throughout Europe, and they embarked on a vigorous war against rebellious princes as well as suppressing the Protestant doctrine within their own lands. This went on for decades, interspersed with a few uneasy truces, and culminated in 1618–1648 with the Thirty Years' War, which proved a disaster for the Germans as a people. Bloodshed, rapine, and destruction haunted the land for decades, and atrocities took place that presaged the horrors of the 20th century. In 1631, to take just one example, two-thirds of the 20,000-strong population of Magdeburg were slaughtered after a successful months-long siege. The biggest losers of the Thirty Years' War were the religious minorities everywhere. Austrian Protestants either reconverted or fled, leaving the country once more largely Catholic.

The next challenge came in July 1683 from the Ottoman Empire, an Islamic power with a large and efficient army that controlled most of southeastern Europe. Some 150,000 Turkish troops massed along the Danube to assault Vienna. The Habsburgs appealed for aid, and the King John Sobieski of Poland agreed to send a relief army accompanied by troops from Saxony, Bavaria, and other parts of Germany.

On September 12, Sobieski's army attacked the Turkish lines and after a 15-hour contest broke the Ottoman army completely. Thousands were slaughtered in the ensuing rout, and the Turks were forced to abandon vast hordes of supplies and booty—including, according to legend, several sacks of coffee beans that were used to establish the first of Vienna's famous coffeehouses. The pursuit of the Turks continued beyond Vienna. Soon Sobieski's forces had pushed the Ottomans out of Hungary completely, and Emperor Leopold was able to make good on an old Habsburg claim to the kingdom of Hungary.

The Habsburg Zenith

In the century that followed the Thirty Years' War, Austria confirmed its place as one of Europe's so-called Great Powers in a series of coalition wars involving France, England, Russia, and a new upstart German kingdom, Prussia. The long years of war began in 1700 when the last king of the Spanish Habsburg line died without leaving an heir. The Austrian Habsburgs had a good legal claim to the inheritance, and it looked for a while as if the great continental empire of Charles V might be resurrected; but Louis XIV, king of France, intervened to place a candidate from his own family on the throne. The War of the Spanish Succession (1701–1714) began with a brilliant victory for the Austrians and their English allies at the Battle of Blenheim in 1704, but the fighting dragged on for years, and eventually the two sides reached a compromise peace that awarded the Spanish title to Louis XIV's claimant.

Far from enjoying European supremacy, the Habsburgs were very soon contemplating the breakup of their entire dynastic estate. The problems began when it became clear that Emperor Charles VI (1685–1740) would leave no male heir, and the Austrian inheritance would fall to his daughter Maria Theresa (1717–1780). Under the international law of the time

Maria Theresa (1717-1780), became Empress of Austria after the death of Emperor Charles VI left no male heir. She rose to the occasion by fiercely defending Austrian lands against Prussian advances and is credited with instituting significant legal and structural reforms to the archduchy.

it was unclear whether or not a woman could succeed to the Austrian archduchy, and Maria Theresa's father went to considerable trouble to get the formal approval of the other Great Powers in a series of agreements known collectively as the Pragmatic Sanction. Unfortunately, as soon as Charles died in 1740 the young and ambitious king of Prussia, Frederick II (known as Frederick the Great) launched a military offensive against Austria, seeking to take advantage of the confusion to steal the rich province of Silesia from the Habsburgs. This crisis in the midst of personal tragedy might have defeated other monarchs, but Maria Theresa, though hardly brilliant or groomed for power, was a tough customer determined to fight for what she believed was rightfully hers. Austria and Prussia waged two extended wars over control of Silesia, from 1740 to 1748 and again from 1756 to 1763, and although she never successfully regained Silesia, Maria Theresa did decisively confirm her own authority among the leaders of Europe.

As the devoted *Landesmutter,* or mother of the land (and motherhood was a role she took quite seriously—she had 16 children), Maria Theresa also spent her long reign trying to introduce structural and legal reforms within Austria to bring the archduchy into the modern age. These were continued by her successor, Josef II (1741–1790), who was influenced by the prevailing ideas of the "Age of Enlightenment" coming from France. The ideal Enlightenment model of government was that of the so-called enlightened despot, a king who would use his absolute authority in the interests of his subjects, and Josef aspired to play the part in Austria. Carrying this to completion was another matter, as it turned out. Josef's centralization of the government's powers angered the local nobility, who felt that their ancient rights were being trampled upon; his desire to make German the language of the state alienated the Hungarians; and his attempts to reform education on secular lines and increase religious toleration aroused the fury of the Catholic church. Many of these schemes, as well as his plan to abolish serfdom, did not long survive his death.

By then war was brewing once more in Europe. Josef's sister Marie Antoinette, who had become queen of France, was arrested and executed along with her husband, Louis XVI, by Parisian revolutionaries who had taken the ideas of the Enlightenment to another stage. The wars of the French Revolution (1792–1815) brought turmoil and destruction to Europe and saw a brilliant French general-turned-emperor, Napoleon Bonaparte, conquer much of the continent. In 1805 Napoleon smashed the combined Austrian and Russian armies at the Battle of Austerlitz, and the following year he dissolved the ancient Holy Roman Empire, creating in its place a German confederacy loyal to him. Henceforth the Habsburgs had to be satisfied with their Austrian titles alone.

Adopting the old family policy of diplomacy by marriage, Francis I (1792–1835) arranged a wedding between his daughter Maria Louisa and Napoleon. This bought the Habsburgs some time while Emperor Bonaparte overextended himself in Russia, and in the war of liberation of 1813 to 1814, the Napoleonic conquests were freed from French rule. After dispatching the dethroned Bonaparte into exile, the diplomats of Europe met at a congress in Vienna to draw up new maps of Europe and try to establish a permanent peace for the continent.

The Decline and Fall of the Habsburgs

By 1815 the Habsburgs ruled a vast and powerful empire. In addition to the old Austrian archduchy, they also controlled Hungary, the lands that make up the modern Czech Republic and Slovakia, Galicia (now in Poland), northern Italy, Slovenia, and Croatia. For the next 100 years, although they would be involved in some sharp little wars, the Habsburg emperors did not have to face a serious external threat to their territory as they had done from Frederick the Great or Napoleon. But as the 19th century continued on, a much more dangerous problem developed inside their borders. New social forces such as liberalism and nationalism were coming to the fore. The first, which demanded greater political authority for ordinary subjects, was bad enough. But the second was even more ominous because the empire was packed with different nationalities— German, Hungarian, Czech, Slovak, Italian, Polish, Romanian, Serb, and Croat to name just the major ones—and if all these groups insisted on national self-rule, then Austria would simply fall to pieces.

The initial reaction to this was to suppress all attempts at reform, or even the discussion of reform. Metternich (1773–1859), chancellor under Francis I, turned Austria into a virtual police state for nearly 30 years, using his powers to arrest or expel anyone suspected of harboring treacherous liberal or nationalist ideas. The response to this suppression, when it came, was explosive. In 1848—a year of revolutionary turmoil throughout Europe—crowds rioted in Vienna, Prague, and Budapest and forced Metternich himself into exile. The Hungarians declared independence, and it took a Russian army to bring the insurgents back into line. In the midst of this chaos, the incompetent emperor of the moment was quietly removed, and a young Habsburg prince, Franz Josef (1830–1916), was installed on the throne. This proved to be a wise decision. Under Franz Josef's calm tutelage, order and authority were restored in Vienna and throughout the empire, although it was now clear that simple repression alone would not be enough to counter the liberal and national challenges. The Habsburgs would have to accommodate themselves to the new realities of European politics as best they could.

Austria's continued weakness was highlighted in 1866 when Prussia launched a lightning-quick war to determine the mastery of Germany once and for all. Although the Holy Roman Empire was long gone, the German princes had continued to look to Vienna as the natural focus of authority; now the Habsburgs had to concede to their Prussian counterparts, the Hohenzollerns, the right to decide matters in Germany. Austria had already been stripped of its Italian territories in an earlier war with France and Piedmont, and now the Hungarians were demanding greater autonomy, as well. The year after his loss in the Austro-Prussian war, Franz Josef enacted what was called the Compromise of 1867; henceforth Hungary would be an equal partner with Austria within the empire, with its own parliament and political rights. This new Austro-Hungarian Empire, as it was called, solved one problem but opened up many others. The Czechs, Croats, and Serbs now demanded their share of national privileges, too. The long-term survival of such a ramshackle institution was beginning to look grim.

The latter years of Franz Josef's long reign were marked by personal tragedy. His beautiful, haunted wife, Elisabeth ("Sissi," as she was known), grew distant and rarely visited the imperial capital. In 1889 their son and heir, Archduke Rudolf, a mentally unstable alcoholic and drug addict, killed himself and his aristocratic mistress at the remote hunting lodge of Mayerling. Nine years later Sissi herself was murdered by an anarchist assassin. Franz Josef and the new heir, his nephew Franz Ferdinand, were never personally close, and the younger man angered his uncle by marrying an obscure noblewoman instead of a princess of the royal rank. As the 20th century opened and Austria's political problems worsened, it seemed as if only the ever-more frail figure of the old emperor—who was genuinely loved and revered by the vast majority of his subjects—was holding the Austro-Hungarian Empire together.

On June 28, 1914, Franz Ferdinand and his wife went to Sarajevo (now in Bosnia) for a routine ceremonial visit.

Shortly after they arrived, a teenage Serbian schoolboy, Gavrilo Princip, marched up to their car and shot the couple dead. Determined to punish Serbia for what it considered a deliberate act of terrorism, Austria declared war and in so doing sparked off World War I (1914–1918) between the "Central Powers" of Germany, Turkey, Bulgaria, and Austria herself and the "Entente Powers" of France, Great Britain, Russia, and eventually the United States.

Millions of men fought and died across Europe in the most dreadful conditions, straining each combatant nation to its limits of endurance. For Austria-Hungary, the strain proved fatal. In November 1916 Emperor Franz Josef died peacefully, and with him died the last ties of loyalty within the Habsburg realm. By the autumn of 1918, rebellious national movements were appearing publicly across the empire, demanding the right to independent statehood. On November 11, the day that the Armistice ending the war was signed, the last emperor, Charles (1887–1922), formally abdicated the imperial throne and left Vienna for the final time. Over 600 years of Habsburg rule in Austria were over.

As the Habsburgs retreated into history, the victorious Entente Powers met near Paris to decide upon the fate of the old Austro-Hungarian Empire. On September 10, 1919, Austrian representatives signed the Treaty of St. Germain (named for the palace it was presented in), which carved up the Habsburg territories into nation-states: Czechoslovakia was formed from Bohemia, Moravia and Slovakia; Galicia became part of the new Republic of Poland; Croatia and Bosnia joined Serbia in the Yugoslav union; Hungary, itself shorn of much territory, became an independent nation. "What's left," said the French prime minister Georges Clemenceau, "is Austria". The predominantly German-speaking peoples in the western end of the old Habsburg estate were left to their own devices, to establish for the first time in their history their own federal republic. Aside from the brief period of union with Germany immediately before and during World War II, Austria has remained an independent state ever since the Treaty of St. Germain. But it has not been an easy journey from empire to modern democratic nationhood.

The grand dome of St. Peter's Church in Vienna reflects the power and influence of the Catholic Church in Austria. About three-quarters of Austria's population are Roman Catholic.

4

The Austrians

In September 1991 a mummified body was discovered preserved in glacial ice in the Ötzal range of the Austrian Alps, close to the Italian border. After being carefully extracted to avoid damage, the frozen corpse was transferred to the University of Innsbruck, where researchers used radiocarbon techniques to try to identify its age. They determined that the man, who was between 25 and 50 when he died and who became affectionately known as "Ötzi" after his final resting place, was around 5,000 years old and had been on a hunting expedition when he met his unfortunate end. Ötzi soon became the subject of an international row between Austria and Italy because the Italians claimed that he rightly belonged to them. His body was transferred to an archeological museum in the Italian city of Bolzano. It was highly symbolic that Ötzi's citizenship should be so ambiguous, because the very nature—and even existence—of

Austrian identity has always been a matter of great controversy. It seems that even the very first Austrian does not know if he is really Austrian at all.

Austrian Society

In the last 50 years Austria's social makeup has gone through the same kinds of changes that most economically and politically conservative societies experienced during their industrialization and urbanization, with some special features reflecting the region's peculiar history and traditions.

Austria in the later years of the Habsburg emperors had a very inflexible social structure, with a tiny clique of aristocrats at the top, a somewhat larger group of "burghers," or middle-class city and town dwellers, below them, and at the base a mass of free peasant-farmers. Movement from one class to the next was unthinkable, and most people considered these social divisions as permanent and rigid facts of life. The only notice-able change was the development of an industrial working class in the empire's cities, like Vienna, but even these became tightly knit and insular communities. The conservative attitude continued to some extent into the early years of the First Republic, and the political turmoil of the interwar period encouraged a so-called *Lager,* or camp, mentality within each group, expressed in fierce parliamentary divisions: The workers of Vienna united behind the Social Democrats, while the farmers and burghers of the provinces adhered to the Christian Social movement. Political allegiances were expressed in every form of life, even in recreational activities like sports, hiking, and music so that, for example, Viennese workers would join socialist swimming and mountain-climbing clubs.

It was only following World War II that important fractures began to appear in this rigid model. As agriculture declined and more working-class Austrians entered the ranks of white-collar management and service jobs, the old simplicities of the social order crumbled. Education, once the exclusive preserve of the rich and privileged, became a means of social advancement.

Family life also altered during the postwar years, as did the roles and opportunities available to Austrian women. The decades immediately following the war were a period of great enthusiasm for the "nuclear family" of young married couples with one or two children living away from elderly parents, in contrast to the old "extended family" in which adult children were expected to take a much larger role in caring for older relatives. The nuclear-family model itself started to break down during the 1960s and 1970s as new ideas about divorce, single-parenthood, and women following professional careers rather than being stay-at-home mothers entered the popular consciousness. Surprisingly, the increasing numbers of children born outside marriage were as accepted in the conservative western provinces of Austria as they were in liberal Vienna. The Alpine regions had a long tradition of tolerance toward illegitimate children because the poor prospects of rural mountain life had always made marriage a difficult and prohibitively expensive rite, and raising "unofficial" families had long been part of local custom.

To American eyes, Austria seems both more and less socially conservative than the modern United States. Austrians, as we shall see, have a more casual attitude toward certain social taboos, and their understanding of issues like the rights of women are more sweeping in scope—for example, Austrian law supports "equal treatment" rather than "equal rights" for women, providing such extra benefits as wage compensation for house-wives working in the home. But the Austrian social structure, for all of its recent loosening, remains more rigid than in North America. Traces of the Lager mentality remain even today.

Attitudes and Beliefs

"National character" is a concept that has to be treated with great caution. Every one of Austria's eight million citizens is an individual with his and her own tastes and attitudes, and to try

to lump these vastly different mind-sets under a single definition risks caricature. But the Austrians themselves believe that
they possess a collective national character, and people from
abroad who have visited or lived in Austria often attest to what
they consider a unique Austrian approach to life.

This national character is paradoxical. On the one hand
Austria is seen as a land of conformism, of rigid adherence to
authority and conventional social graces. Austrians, at least in
public, tend to dress, behave, and talk in a prescribed way that
sometimes strikes outsiders as stuffy or dull. Austrians use the
formal *Sie* form of address rather than the informal *du* more
often than other German speakers. College students in Austria
strike their North American counterparts as far more buttoned
up and serious than would be normal in the United States and
Canada. Austria is sometimes described as the natural home of
the civil servant, a dreary bureaucratic attitude to life. "Austria
is the face behind the ticket office of the world railway," as Karl
Kraus put it—an image that conjures up petty officialdom and
an obsession with orderliness.

But this is only half the story. Austrians might sometimes
display a drab exterior to outsiders, but this can conceal an
emotionally stormy soul and a taste for the eccentric or even
bizarre. The country has an unusually high suicide rate (about
twice the U.S. figure) that it has been suggested is a product of
the tension between Austrians' public staidness and their inner
Sturm und Drang (literally "storm and stress," or turmoil).
While Austrians might appear humorless to foreigners, many
of them share a dry sense of the absurd that is easy to miss.
They are certainly not prudish when it comes to sexual mores;
prostitution is legal throughout Austria, and nudism is openly
practiced in many tourist resorts. For all their formal attire in
the office, Austrians are often accused of being daydreamers
and lacking a strong entrepreneurial spirit. This lack of zeal at
work is sometimes blamed on *Gemütlichkeit*, a word not easily
translated but that means an easygoing attitude toward life that

Austrians supposedly share—a warm private conviviality very different from the sober face they present to the world. Austria is a case where appearances can be very deceptive.

Religiously, the country remains predominantly Roman Catholic, with about three-quarters of all Austrians officially recognized as members of the church. The senior Catholic authorities in Austria tarnished their reputation in the 1920s and 1930s through a close association with the increasingly authoritarian Christian Social Party, and since World War II its churchmen have remained mostly aloof from party politics, with the single exception of the debate on legalizing abortion in the 1970s. Of the religious minorities, about 5 percent is Protestant, a surviving remnant from the persecutions of the Reformation. Only around 7,000 Jews now live in Austria, and these are mostly recent immigrants from the former Soviet Union rather than descendents of Austria's 200,000-strong prewar Jewish community.

It is not easy to tell how strongly religious belief still influences behavior in Austria, nor whether its influence is changing. As a general rule most Austrian Catholics no longer attend regular Mass, and the church's teachings on divorce, contraception, and abortion have largely gone ignored. But Austrians still celebrate the key rites of passage—baptisms, marriages, and funerals—in religious style, and the farther west one goes in the country, the more conventionally spiritual the people tend to be. Although formal affiliation to Catholicism has declined in recent years, this may be partly because Austrian law requires registered churchgoers to pay a "church tax," or a small percentage of their earnings to the church of their choice each year.

Minorities and Immigrants

The Treaty of St. Germain left Austria the most ethnically homogeneous of all the new nation-states formed from the old Habsburg Empire. Approximately 95 percent of the citizens of the new Federal Republic identified themselves as German-speaking. However, there were small groups of indigenous peoples, mostly at the territorial fringes of the country, who were not ethnically German. These included pockets of Slovenes, Croats, Hungarians, Czechs, and Slovaks. These minorities remain to the present-day and are now protected by an Ethnic Groups Law passed in 1976 that forbids discrimination on grounds of ethnicity and mandates bilingual education in the appropriate regions.

However, all the indigenous communities have shrunk greatly in size, at least according to Austrian census returns. In the 1930s and the Nazi era this was because of coercion to assimilate and become "Aryanized"; now the decrease has more to do with the attraction of modern lifestyles, which encourage young people to abandon their traditional ethnic identities and become part of mass consumer society. One indigenous group that has never been officially recognized by the state is the so-called Gypsy people—divided into the Roma and the Sinti—who have for centuries lived throughout eastern and southeastern Europe in semiautonomous, tightly knit village communities. Austrian Gypsies were all but exterminated during World War II, but in recent years they have gained in number and once more exist in a somewhat tense relationship with the rest of the country.

Unlike, say, the United States, Austria has never defined itself as a nation of immigrants. However, the huge increase in the number of citizens and legal residents born outside the country's borders has been one of Austria's most important social and political developments of the last 60 years. To properly understand its importance, we need first of all to appreciate the shifts in Austria's population structure since the First Republic.

Austria underwent a demographic revolution in the years immediately before and after World War II. The country's domestic instability during the 1930s and the Anschluss with

World War II marked a dark period in Austrian history. Nazi annexation claimed Austria as part of Hitler's Reich in 1938. Here, Nazi police march through the streets of Irnst. Over 200,000 Austrians chose to live in exile rather than to live under Nazi rule.

Nazi Germany encouraged over 200,000 Austrian citizens to leave for foreign exile. Around 300,000 Austrians were killed during the war, either while serving on the front lines or as casualties of strategic bombing, and another 100,000 were murdered by the Nazis for political or racial reasons, many of

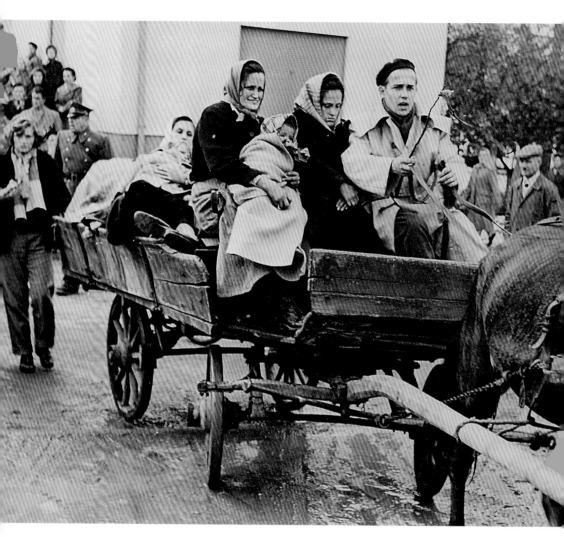

Russia's crackdown on the Hungarian Revolution in 1956 caused waves of refugees to attempt to enter Austria. Russian tanks blockaded Austrian and Hungarian roads and set up checkpoints.

whom perished in the Holocaust. In the period 1945–1950, nearly 500,000 refugees or "displaced persons" from elsewhere in Europe—predominantly German-speaking people from regions occupied by the Soviet Union—came to live in Austria. The country's position as a neutral borderline state between the two Cold War alliances made it a natural destination for people seeking political or economic security; between the end of World War II and the fall of the Berlin Wall in 1989 it is reckoned that up to 2.6 million foreign émigrés passed through Austria at some point or another. The majority of these refugees, mostly from Eastern Europe and the USSR, did not permanently settle in Austria, but hundreds of thousands eventually did.

Austria accepted this role as one of the population highways of the world partly to make restitution for its involvement in Nazi crimes against humanity but also for more practical reasons. The fall in Austria's indigenous population through death and political crisis put serious limits on its available manpower during postwar reconstruction. Although Austria experienced a baby boom during the 1950s and early 1960s like many other western countries, this alone was insufficient to provide a large enough native workforce for the country's growing industrial base. Moreover, by the 1970s the combination of an increasing life expectancy and a dramatically falling birthrate meant that the population was aging fast and badly in need of an additional labor source. So many foreign immigrants were invited into the country to provide a vital contribution to the manpower pool. "Guest workers" from Yugoslavia and Turkey, who did not become naturalized Austrian citizens but who were issued work visas, were also encouraged to emigrate. By the early 1990s around 1 in 10 of Austria's eight million population had been born abroad, and there were up to half a million guest workers in the country, concentrated in Vienna and other large industrial cities.

It was around this time that changes in the Austrian economy, requiring fewer unskilled workers, and fears that the liberation of Eastern Europe from communism would produce a mass inflow of illegal immigrants caused the Austrian government to revise its previously liberal nationality and refugee laws. Troops were called in to seal the borders, and the number of guest-worker visas issued was steadily reduced. The growth of right-wing organizations like the Freedom Party of Austria (FPÖ, discussed in more detail in Chapter 5), feeding on resentment of immigrants and foreigners, has played a major role in Austrian parliamentary politics for over a decade now. Defenders of the immigrants argue that Austria's aging and shrinking indigenous population can only afford to maintain its expensive welfare-state system with the contribution of outside labor, and therefore Austria has a responsibility to maintain its tradition of tolerance for those fleeing persecution and economic woe. But surveys suggest that many people, especially older Austrians in the more socially conservative west, are hardening their attitudes toward immigration.

Who are the Austrians?

The early 20th-century historian and philosopher Oswald Spengler once wrote: "The Austrians feel foreign inside themselves to all other Germans." He was writing this at a time when, as we have seen, "Austria" meant something rather different to what it does now. In those days Austria was at the center of a much larger multinational empire of which the nine provinces of modern Austria were just a minor subsection, although Vienna was the imperial capital. So when someone before World War I referred to "Austrians," they could mean several different things, depending on the context: They might be talking about the provinces of Lower and Upper Austria or the empire's German-speaking peoples or everyone living in the half of the empire directly administered from Vienna— many of whom were not ethnically German—or they could mean something else entirely. The rulers of imperial Austria, who had nothing to gain and everything to lose from nationalism, did their best to subdue any ideas about a distinct Austrian self-consciousness.

So was Spengler right? The creation of an independent Austrian nation-state set off a crisis of identity that to some extent has continued on to the present-day. Essentially, the question each generation of Austrians has had to ask itself is: Are we a unique people with our own collective personality, or are we simply part of a much larger German-speaking cultural community without any distinctive characteristics of our own? Evidence can be assembled on both sides. Take language, for instance. The vast majority of Austrians speak German, tying them intimately to the other German-speaking peoples of Europe. On the other hand the many dialects of German spoken in Austria are rather unusual, often incorporating words from Italian and the Slavic languages and not easily understood by, say, the *Hochdeutsch* (High German) speakers from the Federal Republic of Germany to the north. Language is both a tie and a division.

The question may be a sterile one. Austrians, one could argue, are both Austrian *and* German—culturally at least—and they have successfully created a prosperous, democratic, and much admired home for themselves on that basis. Another writer interested in Austrian national identity, Oskar Bender, said: "To be Austrian is not a geographical concept but a spiritual idea, the idea of an ethnically enlightened humanity springing from a combination of peoples and classes." Many Austrians would agree with that—at least as an inspirational goal.

Since its construction in 1883, the Parliament building in Vienna has been at the heart of Austria's political life. It remains the home of Austria's two legislative houses.

5

The Austrian Republic

As we saw at the end of Chapter 3, modern Austria was forged from the German-speaking remnants of the old Habsburg Empire at the close of World War I. Since the Treaty of St. Germain in 1919, Austria has been a federal republic, governed by a president and parliament in Vienna but with important powers also delegated to its nine self-governing *Länder,* or provinces: Burgenland, Carinthia, Lower Austria, Upper Austria, Salzburg, Styria, Tyrol, Vienna, and Vorarlberg. To be more accurate, there have been two federal republics—the first lasting until 1938, when the country was absorbed into Nazi Germany, and the second beginning in 1955 and continuing to the present day. Despite this break in its political continuity, the Austria of today is still largely governed by the principles laid down in its 1920 constitution, with the most important amendments being made in 1929. To better understand the often-turbulent story of the two republics, it would be useful to analyze the structure of the Austrian government more closely.

Austria's Political System

The Austrian head of state is the federal president, elected by popular vote every six years. This president nominally appoints the government and is commander in chief of the national armed forces. In practice, it is the president's chancellor—usually the leader of the largest political party at the time—who governs the country on a day-to-day basis, appoints a cabinet of ministers, and introduces new legislation in parliament. Parliament is composed of two houses, the lower chamber, or National Council *(Nationalrat)* and the upper chamber, or Federal Council *(Bundesrat)*. The Nationalrat, which has 183 members and is elected by popular vote on a four-year basis, is the more important of the two, and although a new law must be approved by both houses before it becomes official, the Nationalrat can override the vote of the Bundesrat if it so chooses. Nationalrat elections are organized on the principle of "proportional representation," or PR, meaning that the number of members each party obtains is roughly equal to its share in the popular vote. (Congressional elections in the United States are not conducted using PR, which means that there can sometimes be a discrepancy between the number of votes a party receives and the seats that it wins).

The Bundesrat's 64 members are appointed by regional assemblies, or *Landtags,* and its role is to safeguard the rights of Austria's provinces. Membership in the Bundesrat is apportioned according to the population in each province. Each province has a governor in its own right, appointed by the local Landtag, except for Vienna, where the city's mayor also acts as the governor. The Lantags are in turn elected by popular ballot. Each province has its own constitution and can raise taxes as well as organize the local police force, administer primary education, run the region's health and housing services, and implement environmental-protection laws. The provinces fiercely guard their constitutional privileges, and throughout Austria's recent history there has sometimes been tension between the wishes of the federal government in Vienna and the local governors and Landtags.

Austria is a fully functioning modern democracy in which the powers of the government are monitored and, if necessary, restricted by an independent judicial system. The Constitutional Court, whose 13 members are directly appointed by the federal president, is the supreme legal authority in the country and, if need be, can overturn a parliamentary law if it is deemed to be contrary to the national constitution. A whole series of lower courts handle ordinary civil and criminal matters, although in situations involving fundamental liberties, an ordinary citizen may be able to appeal his case all the way to the Constitutional Court. Austria has a professional civil service, which is independent of party political allegiance and helps to administer the country efficiently.

The two most powerful political parties in the Republic are the Social Democratic Party (SPÖ) and the Austrian People's Party (ÖVP). Both can trace their origins to the Habsburg period, and they reflect the key ideological and geographical divisions within Austrian society. The SPÖ, a left-wing party espousing broadly socialist principles, has traditionally derived most of its electoral support from the working-class population of Vienna and other large cities. By contrast, the ÖVP is more politically conservative and is strongest in the small-town middle class and the mountainous western provinces. During their earlier history, these two parties were bitter parliamentary foes, even taking their conflicts onto the street with violent results, but nowadays their differences are more of degree than of kind. For example, modern Social Democrats tend to support Austria's heavily nationalized and state-controlled industrial system, while the People's Party is more skeptical about the benefits of government intervention in the economy. Both parties have gone through name and image changes because of embarrassing associations with Austria's political past. During most of the postwar period, the SPÖ was officially called the Socialist Party, but it returned to its older Social Democratic title after the collapse of communism in Eastern Europe because it did not want to be too closely identified with the failed Soviet system. Similarly, the ÖVP started life as the Christian Social Party but abandoned this name after World War II because it had been tarnished by involvement with the Nazis.

The political mood of 21st-century Austria stands in marked contrast to the bitterness and rancor that characterized the First Republic. Both the Social Democrats and the People's Party have wanted above all to avoid the political instability that undid their country in 1938, and because the proportional representation system makes it difficult for one party alone to control the Nationalrat, they have often governed together in so-called Grand Coalitions. A policy of *Proporz* (proportionality) is used in such cases, whereby positions in government are tacitly allotted to each side in rough proportion to their electoral support. This discourages political infighting and has aided the country's peaceful postwar development, but critics have charged that it weakens the authority of parliament and has brought corruption into government. The rise of the right-wing Freedom Party of Austria (FPÖ) can partly be traced to dislike of the influence of Proporz in Austrian politics.

Another feature of Austria's political system is the so-called social partnership between the government, management, and labor, expressed in institutions like the Wage-Price Commission. This commission meets to negotiate changes in wages and prices between representatives of the state, employers, and trade-union leaders and is intended to keep the Austrian economy healthy through compromise and mutual agreement rather than competition. The social partnership reflects the determination of Austrian's mainstream politicians to avoid the destructive power struggles within their society that characterized the ill-fated First Republic. However, some Austrians have complained that the partnership is similar to the Proporz system, rewarding establishment favorites at the expense of the general public.

The First Republic (Up to 1938)

After 1919 the new Austrian nation was beset with problems. Food shortages and unemployment were rampant, and the local currency suffered massive inflation. The creation of a short-lived Bolshevik regime in neighboring Hungary brought fears of a Communist *putsch*, or revolt. Perhaps most serious of all, many Austrians lacked any unifying sense of allegiance to their new republic. In imperial times the Habsburg emperors had represented the symbolic center of patriotism; now, with no binding sentiment to keep the country together, what alternative focus of loyalty was there? Indeed, many people in Austria believed that the best course their country could take would be *Anschluss,* or unification, with their fellow German speakers to the north (in the postwar Weimar Republic). But the Entente Powers had specifically forbidden Anschluss between Austria and Germany in the terms of the Treaty of St. Germain, and in the immediate aftermath of World War I, neither country was in any position to defy that ban.

Politically there was little room for compromise between the Social Democrats and their Christian Social opponents. The Christian Social Party led a conservative coalition that ran the federal government from 1920 up to the end of democratic politics in the first Republic 14 years later, but it was never able to establish firm control over the parliamentary life of the country. Vienna, which had important state powers of its own, remained the stronghold of the Social Democrats, who implemented a series of ambitious social reforms during the 1920s. "Red Vienna," as it became known, saw the construction of large and elaborate housing projects for city workers that influenced urban planners across the world.

Conflict between left and right was expressed not only through political means but also by violence. Conservative radicals created the *Heimwehr,* a paramilitary force intended to suppress left-wing agitators that eventually became a fascist political party, while the socialists countered with a militia of their own, the *Schutzbund.* Both of these groups engaged in bloody street clashes with one another, and their existence served to undermine the already fragile democratic tradition in Austria. Ignaz Seipel (1876–1932), a former Jesuit priest and college professor who served as Austria's chancellor throughout most of the 1920s, increasingly relied upon the Heimwehr to maintain political control. In July 1927, on a day later known as Black Friday, a demonstration by Viennese workers was brutally broken up by the authorities, and in the ensuing chaos nearly 100 people were killed and the Ministry of Justice Building burned down. Another troubling development on the political stage was the emergence of an Austrian National Socialist ("Nazi") movement, mimicking the German organization under the leadership of Adolf Hitler.

In 1932 a new Christian Social politician, Engelbert Dollfuss (1892–1934), became federal chancellor. Dollfuss came to power shortly after the collapse of the Austrian banking system had ushered in a new economic slump. He believed that democratic politics had failed in Austria and that only an authoritarian regime could recreate stability in the country. In March 1933, taking advantage of a procedural problem in the Austrian government, Dollfuss suspended parliament and later that year announced the creation of the "Fatherland Front," a coalition of conservative parties intended to keep the socialists from any chance of power. Although Dollfuss was now effectively a right-wing dictator—the period of his rule is sometimes called Austro-Fascism—he distrusted the Austrian Nazis and was as keen to suppress them as the communists. Dollfuss also feared that Hitler, who had now become German chancellor, would try to seize Austria by force, and so he sought alliance with the Italian dictator Benito Mussolini. Although Mussolini would later ally with the Germans during the World War II, in 1933 he was eager to restrain Hitler's ambitious plans, and so he agreed to support Dollfuss on condition that the Fatherland Front crack down on the Viennese Social Democrats.

Tensions came to a head the following year when first the Social Democrats and then the Austrian Nazis revolted. The left-wing uprising in February 1934 was poorly organized, and the government was able to quickly regain control, although hundreds of working-class militiamen were killed and wounded in the fighting. In July the Nazis seized control of the chancellor's office in an attempt to overthrow the regime; Dollfuss was shot and died soon after, and it was left to a new leader, Kurt Schuschnigg (1897–1977), to reassert authority. Using the Heimwehr, Schuschnigg ordered the arrest and execution of leading Nazis; the putsch had failed. The outcome of the 1934 crisis was the forced dissolution of all political parties except the Fatherland Front. In 1935 Great Britain, France, and Italy came together in what was known as the Stresa Front in a demonstration of support for Austrian independence. It looked for a moment as if Austria might achieve some kind of diplomatic security.

Unfortunately for Schuschnigg, the unity of the Stresa Front was short-lived because Italy alienated Great Britain and France by invading Ethiopia in 1936. At home, by trying to fight the Social Democrats and the Nazis at the same time, Schuschnigg's government isolated and weakened itself. By early 1938 Hitler felt strong enough to renew German designs on Austria. Under pressure from Hitler, Schuschnigg agreed to bring some Austrian Nazis into the government, but clearly agitation for Anschluss was growing within the country and outside. On March 9 Schuschnigg attempted to forestall unification by announcing a referendum on the continued existence

Federal Chancellor Kurt Schuschnigg, shown in 1935. Schuschnigg's efforts to prevent German annexation of Austria were successful until he lost the support of Italian leader Benito Mussolini. Schuschnigg became a Nazi prisoner until 1945. After the war, he settled in the United States and taught at St. Louis University until his death in 1977.

of Austria. Hitler immediately demanded that he abandon this plan, and, defeated, Schuschnigg agreed. Two days later German troops invaded Austria in a bloodless occupation, and on March 15 Hitler appeared in Vienna to ecstatic crowds to announce the Anschluss. Austria's brief experiment with independence had ended—for the time being.

Reaction to the Anschluss was mixed. Many thousands of Austrians chose to leave their country rather than accept Nazi government, and Austria lost the talents of some of its most famous and gifted sons and daughters, including Sigmund Freud. Others disliked the arrangement, though they tolerated it. But for many people the desire for Anschluss had lingered ever since the creation of the Republic at the end of World War I; they were also attracted to the economic prosperity and stability that Germany seemed to promise. Although after 1945 Austrians sometimes pretended otherwise, at the time millions of them greeted absorption into Hitler's Third Reich with enthusiasm.

The group with the most to fear from the Anschluss was, of course, Austria's Jewish population, which was concentrated in the capital. Its local heritage was deeply rooted; there is evidence that Jews had been living in Vienna since Roman times, and in 1938 the city's Jewish community was around 170,000 strong. Austrian Jews had long experienced forms of official and unofficial anti-Semitism—some mild and some not so mild—but their community had also played a major role in Vienna's artistic, business, and professional life, and many of the city's wealthiest and most respected citizens were Jewish. The effects of the Anschluss were devastating. Tens of thousands hurriedly emigrated in the wake of Nazi rioting that was even more vicious than in Germany itself, and most of the 33,000 Jewish businesses in Vienna were broken up or forcibly taken over. Some 65,000 Viennese Jews would die in the ensuing Holocaust.

The Second Republic (1945 and After)

A little more than a year after the Anschluss, Hitler's Reich was at war with Great Britain and France. Soon the Soviet Union and, later, the United States joined the fight against Nazism. By 1945 Germany had been defeated, and—echoing 1918—the Allies once again had to decide what to do with Austria. The immediate decision was to partition the country into four areas of occupation—American, British, French, and Russian—with Vienna additionally being divided into four areas and a central "international zone." A provisional government was installed, led by Karl Renner (1870–1950), who had also been the first chancellor of Austria in 1918. Renner included former members of the Social Democrat and Christian Socialist parties, the latter now reorganizing itself as the Austrian People's Party. But real authority remained in the hands of the occupying powers. The atmosphere of the immediate postwar period is captured in *The Third Man,* a well-known 1949 movie set in Vienna starring Orson Welles.

The onset of the Cold War between the western powers and the Soviet Union made progress on the Austrian question more complicated. Austrians feared that the division of their country into zones might become permanent, as had happened in Germany. The key to ensuring a continued unified Austria was to offer a guarantee of neutrality in the competition between East and West. In May 1955, the Austrian State Treaty was signed by the occupying powers, creating the Second Austrian Republic and returning the country to the status of an independent and sovereign nation. Austria had to agree not to attempt any further Anschluss with Germany, forego any political alliances with either side of the so-called Iron Curtain, and make hefty payments to the Soviet Union for the return of goods and property confiscated at the end of the Second World War.

During the 1950s and 1960s Grand Coalitions generally governed the country. In 1970, however, the socialists under Bruno Kreisky (1911–1990) won their own majority and proceeded to run Austria alone for the next 13 years. "King Bruno," as he was known to many Austrians, dominated the political life of the country throughout the 1970s and early 1980s. His tenure as chancellor saw the extension of Austria's generous social-welfare state and the democratization of important Austrian institutions like the university system. A political moderate, Kreisky worked to broaden the electoral appeal of his party and also went to great pains to distance his socialist beliefs from those practiced in communist Eastern Europe. A series of financial scandals in 1983 dethroned the king, and he resigned under something of a black cloud.

The Freedom Party and the Legacy of Anschluss

By far the most contentious aspect of Austria's political life today has been the rise of a third party to challenge the Social Democrats and the People's Party, namely the Freedom Party of Austria, or FPÖ.

The FPÖ was formed in 1956 and attracted a motley crew of old-fashioned conservatives, extreme nationalists, and even former Nazis—who in some cases did not disguise their continued sympathies for National Socialism. Although at first a minor force, the FPÖ successfully tapped into popular resentment both of the corruption scandals that were plaguing Austrian politics in the 1970s and 1980s and of the increasing numbers of foreign-born immigrants to the country. Their first taste of power came in 1983, when Bruno Kreisky stood down. The socialists, who had suffered losses in recent elections, needed a coalition partner to retain control of the government and, in a surprise move, offered a place to the FPÖ. In 1986 the Freedom Party also gained an effective new leader, Jörg Haider (1950–). However, that year the socialists abandoned the alliance, and in 1987 they recreated the old Grand Coalition with the People's Party.

The reason for this sudden switch in tactics was the election to the Austrian presidency in 1986 of Kurt Waldheim (1918–), the Austrian Republic's most internationally well-known politician. Waldheim, the secretary-general of the United Nations from 1971 to 1981, was suddenly accused during his presidential campaign of covering up his involvement in Nazi atrocities during his wartime service in Yugoslavia. Waldheim's evasive responses to questioning deepened suspicion among many that he was being less than candid about his past.

Former U.N. Secretary General Kurt Waldheim was inaugurated as Austria's President in 1986. Controversy surrounded Waldheim regarding the extent of his involvement with the Nazis while serving in the German army during World War II.

Waldheim's election set off a storm of protest across the international community, and the United States declared that the Austrian president was an "undesirable" who would not be allowed to enter the country—a major diplomatic snub. For the five years of Waldheim's term, Austria found itself effectively isolated.

Waldheim's election and the increasing success of the FPÖ touched a raw nerve within Austrian society. Was the president's hedging about his past representative of the Austrian attitude to the Third Reich—that the country had chosen to forget its former enthusiasm for Hitler's regime by portraying itself as a victim of German policies rather than their executor? And did nostalgia for National Socialism continue to linger in Austria?

In recent years many Austrians have gone to considerable lengths to dispel this belief. In October 2000 the government finalized an agreement to pay compensation to 150,000 former slave laborers who were pressed into service during World War II, at a cost of over $400 million. Plus in January 2001 Austria agreed to create a compensation program for the property stolen from its Jewish populace in the Nazi era. And as we saw in Chapter 4, postwar Austria has accepted huge numbers of refugees fleeing war or tyranny in their own countries—an act of generosity that ironically has served to embitter some native Austrians and foster the support of the Freedom Party.

The controversy made world news once again in October 1999 when the Grand Coalition of the socialists and the People's Party broke down, and after much parliamentary wrangling the People's Party offered Haider's FPÖ (which had won 27 percent of the popular vote in recent elections) a new role in government. This quickly became known as the "black-blue coalition"—black and blue being the respective colors of the ÖVP and the FPÖ—and it provoked hostility both inside the country and abroad. Massive demonstrations by protestors took place throughout Austria, and the European Union (EU), which Austria joined in 1995, implemented diplomatic sanctions against the new government in Vienna. The black-blue coalition denounced the sanctions as interference in Austria's internal affairs, but its leaders also agreed to sign a statement rejecting racial discrimi- nation and allowed observers from the European Commission on Human Rights to report on the democratic state of Austrian politics. This report, as well as Haider's resignation as head of the FPÖ in February 2000, eased concerns somewhat, and the EU lifted its sanctions. But the continuing presence of the FPÖ in Austrian government remains a sore point in the country's relationship with the outside world.

Modern nightlife and ancient culture exist side-by-side on Vienna's Kartnerstrasse.

6

Austria's Economy

In May 1931 the Creditanstalt, one of Austria's oldest and most important banks, collapsed under a mountain of debt. In other small countries the ruin of a big banking concern might have caused some local economic problems, but it probably would not have precipitated a major world crisis. The Creditanstalt failure, however, was different. Austria lay at the heart of Europe's intricate financial web—a web that had been dangerously frayed by the Wall Street crash of the New York Stock Exchange in 1929. The repercussions from the collapse of the Creditanstalt were devastating. Other European banks began to topple and fall, and the panic spread across the Atlantic to North America. Soon, the entire world was in the grip of an economic malaise that became known as the Great Depression, the slump that in part brought about the rise of the dictatorial regimes of Europe and Asia and the outbreak of World War II.

Thankfully, Austria's role in the world economy has rarely been as catastrophic as it was in 1931. But the fall of the Creditanstalt is a dramatic example of Austria's importance to the international financial community. Despite its modest size, Austria's location and resources have long been vital to European economic development. Historically, Austria has gone through a long and—at times painful—transition from a mainly agricultural to a high-tech capitalist base, and in the 21st century it faces new challenges as it adjusts to the changing economic realities of globalization and the decline of old heavy industries.

Land and Resources

As you might imagine, a country as festooned with mountains and forests as Austria has never been an easy place to develop economically. This is not to say that the Alpine lands are without value, however. On the contrary, Austria has many useful economic resources such as metals, minerals, timber, and even oil and gas. The problem for Austrians throughout history has not so much been the scarcity of useful raw materials as the difficulty of extracting them from a challenging terrain; the areas richest in assets have often been hardest to utilize.

By the sixth century B.C. settlers were mining the salt deposits in the Salzburg region, from which the name of the province derives. It was however copper, and above all iron, which attracted early entrepreneurs like the Romans to Austria; the famous Iron Mountain (Erzberg) in Styria, made almost entirely of its namesake metal, has been strip mined for centuries for its valuable ores. In more recent years Austria's hillsides have also yielded magnesite (a key ingredient in modern chemistry), lead, lignite, and zinc. The thick belts of forest covering these hills can also be used for timber and paper.

Austria has several important energy resources, though not nearly enough to sustain the huge demands of its modern economy. Although some petroleum and natural gas deposits have been discovered in the eastern part of the country, and it is estimated that the whole region north of the Alps may lie on top of a vast underground oil field that could one day be tapped, for the time being Austria still has to import most of its petrol, coal, and gas supplies from abroad. Electricity is a different story, however. About two-thirds of Austria's electric supply comes from a series of ingenious hydro dams, which use the waterpower of the country's lakes and rivers to turn enormous turbines, generating inexpensive and pollution-free electricity.

Agriculture has always been difficult in Austria for practical reasons, and in recent years it has become a thorny political question as well. Only the eastern part of the country, around the Danube Valley, is really suited to traditional arable farming of cereal crops, potatoes, and sugar beets. Farmers in the hillier Alpine regions, where the land is more rugged and difficult to plough, prefer to keep livestock such as pigs, poultry, and cattle. Before World War II a fairly large proportion of the Austrian labor force, especially in the west, was still concentrated in the agricultural sector. After 1945, however, the share of the population living or working on farms dwindled rapidly. Ironically, part of the reason for this is the enormous increase in agricultural productivity that modern farming methods, especially mechanization, have produced; Austria is now capable of supplying all of its own cereal, meat, and milk needs, which has meant that many farming communities have been surplus to requirements and have drifted out of agriculture altogether, switching to tourism for their income.

The postwar decline of the Austrian small farm raised concerns among many citizens that the traditional social fabric of their countryside was in jeopardy. The government in Vienna responded to this by becoming heavily involved in the agricultural industry, setting minimum market prices and providing generous subsidies to farming concerns. This has kept the remaining Austrian rural sector at an artificially stable size, but it has ill-prepared the country's farmers for the challenges of competition from abroad. Austria's complex agricultural regulations were a key sticking point when the country negotiated its entry into the European Union in the 1990s, and they continue to cast a shadow over its relationship with its EU partners. Those Austrian farmers who have found it difficult enough to maintain their traditional pastoral life in an increasingly industrialized and urban society now worry that they will lose the government support that has kept their small family-run farms viable.

Manufacturing and Services

One of the paradoxes about Austria is that a country with such a landscape of wilderness should also be a major conduit of human contact and communication. As we saw earlier, the Austrian Alps are intersected by a series of mountain passes that provide a land bridge between the Baltic and Mediterranean worlds, while the River Danube connects Western Europe to the Balkans and the Black Sea. It is not surprising, then, that Austria has long played a major role in transcontinental trade, with Vienna acting as one of the key commercial centers of medieval Europe. This mercantile heritage provided the foundation for Austria's important role as an industrial and financial hub in the modern era.

Modern Austria is one of the world's most industrious and profitable manufacturing nations. The country makes and exports sophisticated goods like specialized ores, tools, textiles, glass, and porcelain as well as many unique luxury items requiring skilled workers and equipment; about half of all the world's skis are made in Austria, for example, perhaps not surprising given the local demand for them. During the 1950s and 1960s, Austria predominantly invested in traditional heavy industries like steelmaking, and a large proportion of the country's workforce was employed in large smokestack factories, producing industrial goods for engineering and machine works. During and after the 1970s, however, there was a slow

Navigable by barges from Ulm, and by larger craft from Regensburg, the Danube is an important shipping route, with canals linking it to other ports.

but steady global decline in the demand for this kind of production, and the focus of the Austrian economy shifted from metals and chemicals to the "service" sector—industries like retail trade, banking, and telecommunications. This was a difficult transition for a mass workforce used to factory methods, and like many European countries Austria suffered serious unemployment.

One service industry in particular, tourism, is especially important to the modern economy. Austria has the highest per capita income from tourism in Europe, and the country's

Skiing remains a major attraction in the Austrian Alps. Each year, thousands of enthusiasts gather at places like Stubai Glacier to enjoy the sport and the dramatic scenery.

unquestionable natural charms, rich cultural heritage, modern amenities, and central location make it an obvious destination for foreign travelers. Indeed, catering to the world's vacation seekers has become so critical a facet of Austria's economic life that all of its political decisions must take the potential impact on tourism into account. The country's new focus on environmental responsibility has been propelled partly because it was feared that Austria's lucrative beauty spots might be in peril from pollution. Unfortunately, mass tourism tends to create ecological pressures of its own, and so the desire for ever-greater numbers of visitors has to be weighed carefully against Austria's environmental sustainability.

National Industries and Privatization

In 1946 the new postwar Austrian government introduced a nationalization law that put control of the country's 70 most important industrial companies in state hands. The government became the sole owner of Austria's mining, oil refining, and electrical-power industries and also took responsibility for all major banks. In a single sweep, Austria's government now employed one-fifth of the country's labor workforce and soon controlled a higher proportion of national productive output than any other country in Western Europe.

This system of state paternalism has characterized Austria's economy for most of its modern history. It has been a policy with mixed success. Nationalization brought full employment and the guarantee of stability to a people who unsurprisingly ranked economic security highly on their list of wants. During the 1950s and 1960s, while Austria enjoyed rapid economic growth from its postwar ruins, nationalization remained popular with the voters. But as the 1970s ushered in a period of worldwide economic fluctuations caused by an energy crisis and the decline in heavy industrial demand, critics began to voice complaints about the system. It encouraged economic sluggishness and lack of entrepreneurial zest, they claimed, and the managers of the state companies were too closely connected to leading politicians; nationalization was at best inefficient—and at worst corrupt.

Between 1975 and 1985 Austria's ruling Socialist Party (SPÖ) introduced numerous institutional reforms intended to make the country's nationalized industries more cost effective and less beholden to political interests. The collapse of the Soviet Union and the communist Eastern Bloc in 1989 to 1991 and Austria's correspondingly new relationship with the European Union (for which see more below) encouraged even more radical changes, and during the 1990s the process of economic privatization began in earnest. For all of its newfound enthusiasm for the free market, however, Austria remains by Western European standards a country with an unusually large amount of government influence in the economy.

It is ironic in light of all this that Austria's most significant contribution to modern economic theory, the "Austrian School" of economics, is characterized by a distrust of the state. The Austrian School was founded by a group of professors teaching at the University of Vienna at the beginning of the 20th century, and although their individual attitudes varied somewhat, one of the school's overall beliefs was that governments should interfere in the workings of the market economy as little as possible. The most important student of the Austrian School was Friedrich Hayek (1899–1992), a Viennese-trained economist who emigrated to Great Britain during the 1930s. Hayek's famous book, *The Road to Serfdom,* was influenced by developments he witnessed in the Nazi and Communist spheres. He won the Nobel Prize for Economics in 1974.

The "European Question"

Perhaps the most pressing of all Austria's economic problems is its relationship with the European Union, or EU, which it joined in 1995.

The postwar Austrian government was committed to a policy of neutrality during the Cold War between the United States and the Soviet Union. This meant, among other things, that Austria had to avoid becoming involved in entangling political relationships on either side of the Iron Curtain, and this prohibition included membership of the EU—originally known as the European Economic Community, or EEC—founded in 1958 by France, West Germany, Italy, and the "Benelux" countries (Belgium, the Netherlands, and Luxembourg). Although officially concerned only with matters of international trade, from its very beginnings the membership of the EEC had clear political implications, and these became more explicit during the 1970s and 1980s as the organization moved toward greater legal unity between its member states.

In 1960 in place of the EEC, Austria joined what was known as the European Free Trade Association (EFTA), a less closely linked group of states that included Great Britain, Portugal, Switzerland, and the Scandinavian countries. EFTA never really prospered, and as more of its members left to join the EU, Austria found itself more and more economically isolated. This limited Austria's export growth but also allowed it to manage its domestic economy without outside interference.

The end of the Cold War released Austria from its vow of neutrality and opened up the possibility of joining the EU. This initiated an often-rancorous debate within Austria about the country's proper relationship with the rest of Europe, a debate that crossed traditional party lines and created unusual coalitions of left- and right-wing politicians. The public remained skeptical, and the 1995 vote in favor of membership by a 66 percent majority was by no means preordained.

Austria's place within the Union remains an ambivalent one. Membership gives Austrians unprecedented access to one of the richest commercial markets in the world, but it has also required the country to reduce its large budget deficit and deregulate its rigorously controlled financial and energy industries, a process that it still taking place. Integration into the EU opens up the unwelcome prospect of competition from outside, while some Austrians have seen the Haider controversy as an intrusion into their own democratic decision making. The replacement of the schilling with the euro as the country's monetary unit in 2002 will likely heighten these tensions as well as open up new business opportunities. Although Austria has re-entered the mainstream of European economic development, not all Austrians agree as to whether their country really belongs there.

The golden interior of Vienna's opera house attests to a rich musical tradition that includes the Vienna Boys Choir. Vienna's composers have included masters such as Mozart, Beethoven, and Brahms. The opera remains the centerpiece of the city's cultural life.

7

Living in Austria Today

G iven the political and financial uncertainties as well as the physical destruction that their country experienced during parts of the 20th century, modern Austrians appreciate only too well the benefits and security that they now enjoy. Austria today, for all of its occasional problems and failings, is a democratic, prosperous, and tolerant society in which most ordinary citizens can expect a safe and rewarding day-to-day life. The material comforts and opportunities that are standard in the United States are familiar to Austrians, too, although some of the subtler forms of lifestyle are different for historical or cultural reasons. A transplanted American would immediately recognize Austria as a foreign country—but not feel totally out of place there.

Town and Country

The perennial division in Austrian life is between the countryside and the city—"city" here meaning, above all, Vienna, by far the largest of Austria's urban centers and home to 20 percent of the population. The metropolis and the rural provinces that surround it have long shared a mutual misunderstanding—and not a little suspicion; country residents traditionally see Vienna as the home of meddling politicians and soulless bureaucrats, while to city dwellers the Alpine regions are unsophisticated and primitive. There is a grain—but only a grain—of truth in these stereotypes, for Vienna is certainly awash in clerks and government employees, while the lifestyle in the countryside is a little less up-to-date than one would find in the capital. With the coming of mass consumerism and popular culture, however, the differences between the urban and the rural are becoming increasingly narrower.

Vienna is a modern European municipality similar to the great cities of North America. It is a remarkably clean and safe place, with little serious crime and less obvious poverty than would be typical in a big U.S. urban area. Viennese are immensely proud of their home and its celebrated attractions, which include among other tourist magnets the gorgeously decorated 18th-century rococo summer palace at Schönbrunn, the Spanish Riding School with its white Lippizaner horses, and the Reisenrad Ferris wheel, now over 100 years old and still open for business. Shopping in Vienna is more complicated than in America because opening hours are less flexible—stores frequently close for up to two hours at lunchtime—and there are fewer late-night and weekend openings. In some ways the Austrians have never really developed a service-oriented business culture, and this is particularly obvious in the capital where salespeople are not especially inclined to be helpful to their customers. Austrians

Austria's famed Lippizaner horses are famous for their performances at the Spanish Riding School in Vienna. At the close of World War II, U.S. General George Patton took the horses under the care of the U.S. Army, thus saving them from destruction by the Russians who then controlled Austria.

themselves are, of course, accustomed to this, but it can be a shock for the unwary foreign traveler used to more pampering by storekeepers!

Travel both within and beyond Vienna is easy and efficient. Austria boasts an excellent national railroad service that covers all the major towns and cities of the country, and buses are available in rural areas that lack train connections. The interstate (Autobahn) system is extensive and well maintained, though the driving regulations are stricter than in neighboring Germany. Austrians are very fond of cycling, and it is convenient to rent bicycles from railroad stations. Given the country's great natural beauty, travel in Austria is a pleasure in itself, particularly when traversing the Alpine ranges by rail or road.

Austrians who live in the countryside are typically thought to be less staid and withdrawn than their city cousins, their way of life more relaxed and friendly. This convivial attitude has probably been encouraged in recent years by the huge increase in tourism in mountainous and woodland areas. Much of this tourist traffic is homegrown because Austrians enjoy generous vacation time from work—typically five or six weeks a year—and they like to spend holidays in the countryside pursuing leisure activities like skiing and hiking. This has been a huge boon to the rural economy but has also presented a challenge to local social structures. Many small rural settlements have responded to the demand for tourist accommodation by growing out of all proportion to their original size, so that in some cases Alpine villages can have 20 hotel beds for every permanent resident. This rapid seasonal expansion and contraction upsets the pattern of life in the community and makes it difficult to maintain older customs and habits. Nonetheless, some surprisingly old-fashioned mannerisms persist. It is still not unusual, for example, to see Austrians, particularly elderly people in rural areas, going about their everyday business in traditional *Trachten,* or folk costumes, including *lederhosen*—leather shorts—for the men and long, flowing dirndl dresses for the women.

One thing that Austrian city and country dwellers agree on is their collective love of good food—and in great quantities. Austrians typically eat a prodigious amount of delicious but rather unhealthy fare, rich with meats, cheeses, potatoes, and dumplings, which makes the Austrian dinner table a delight but which also contributes to a high national incidence of heart disease and other diet-related health problems. Particular favorites are Wiener schnitzel, a pork or veal cutlet wrapped in fried bread crumbs, and strudel, a succulent apple- and raisin-filled pastry. Wine and coffee are the beverages of choice, and Vienna has a venerable coffeehouse culture of street-side cafés in which to linger and chat.

Education and Welfare

Austrians are rightly proud of their country's free public-education system, which ranks among the best in the world. In addition to other academic studies, most young Austrians acquire a good working knowledge of English. A small private-school sector, predominantly run by the Roman Catholic Church, also boasts many fine schools. Attendance from age 6 to age 15 is mandatory, and the progression from one school to another is complex, but essentially students must decide (or, more realistically, their parents must decide) whether they go forward to a regular secondary school, or *Hauptschule*, in preparation for an industrial apprenticeship or vocational training or to a preparatory *Gymnasium* with the idea to matriculate into a university. This two-track system seems rigid to North Americans, but in fact the present system is a considerably more flexible version of the classic education structure that was even more stratified and effectively restricted university opportunities to the social elite.

The country has 12 universities, a high number in proportion to the relatively small population, and 6 academies of art and music, which reflect Austria's strong high-cultural traditions. The University of Vienna, a medieval institution, is by far the oldest and largest. Since the educational reforms of the 1960s and 1970s, attendance at university has become a mass phenomenon, and the lack of tuition costs—these are borne by the state through taxpayers—means that Austrians

This tinted engraving from 1825 shows the grand structures of the University of Vienna. Founded in 1365, it is the oldest university in the German-speaking world, and continues to be an educational center respected throughout Europe and the world.

can take a much more leisurely, even lifelong approach to higher education. However, the democratization of university entrance has put an inevitable strain on resources, and there is much debate within Austria as to whether academic standards have fallen as a result.

Austria has a comprehensive welfare-state system that seeks to ensure its citizens' health and financial security from cradle to grave. Workers pay national insurance contributions from their wages, which cover the costs of unemployment, sickness, and old-age pensions for all. Employees are also required to join health-insurance plans that provide almost free in- and outpatient treatment in Austria's excellent hospital system. Work benefits are generous, with most wage earners working 40 hours or less a week and receiving five weeks of paid vacation a year. Naturally all of this is very expensive, and one of the challenges facing Austria's political leadership is to maintain the country's popular welfare system in light of an aging population and a dwindling workforce. Social security in particular is in need of reform as more elderly retirees become eligible and fewer young employees become available to support them.

Austrian Festivals and Traditions

As a country with a predominantly Roman Catholic heritage, Austria's annual celebrations are mostly based around the calendar of Christian observances such as Christmas and Easter. There are also celebrations connected to the agricultural cycle, like harvest thanksgiving, and some modern holidays representing more contemporary events. The most important of these is Austria's National Day, October 26, which commemorates the departure of the last Allied occupying troops after World War II and the re-creation of the federal republic.

Austria's most elaborate festival is Fasching, an old Germanic word referring to the last drink supped before a fast. Technically, Fasching takes place on the eve of Ash Wednesday (also known in North America as Fat Tuesday), but in recent years the definition has stretched, and it now also more generally refers to the whole winter period between mid-November and the onset of Lent. Fasching is an Austrian variation on the old European tradition of carnival, in which people would let their hair down and enjoy sump-tuous—and occasionally riotous—public celebrations before beginning the fasting period that precedes Easter. In earlier centuries ordinary people would dress up in masks and costumes and openly mock the nobility and church leaders as a way of letting off steam. An element of the subversive lingers in Fasching even today, but the celebrations have generally become much tamer and more standardized. Hundreds of ornate balls take place in Vienna during the carnival season, while in some rural villages they still stage variations on the old masked Fasching street parades.

Like American children, Austrian boys and girls look forward to the arrival of Santa Claus in December. However, he is known to them as Saint Nicholas, his visit is on December 6 rather than Christmas Eve, and he has in tow a mischievous goatlike companion called Krampus who traditionally represents the devil and whose job it is to give lumps of coal instead of presents to naughty children! Fortunately for Austria's younger citizens, Krampus is not obliged to give out much coal these days, and instead they all receive small gifts and candies from Saint Nicholas. The Christmas period is also marked by festive markets where stallholders sell hot drinks, ornaments, and handcrafted goods, while in the Tyrol there is a tradition of visiting people's homes to view elaborate Nativity cribs with models of the Holy Family, the shepherds, and the three wise men.

Like the Tyrolean crib visiting, many of Austria's most distinctive festival traditions are restricted to small provincial areas. Each year in the Carinthian hamlet of Tressdorf, the local farmers perform a wordless version of the Easter story called the Mölltall passion play, which attracts many curious visitors. Another annual celebration takes place in Neckenmarkt in Burgenland, though there the focus is not religion but historical patriotism: A young boy marches through the town waving the flags of the Hungarian Esterházy dynasty and the Holy Roman Empire in a demonstration of loyalty dating back to the 17th century. In

Salzburg and Styria some villages build large wooden and paper models of the Biblical strongman Samson, who is then proudly borne around on church parades and ceremonies. It has been suggested that this tradition started as a way of scaring off invading Turkish soldiers.

Arts and Leisure

Austria has a magnificent artistic heritage that is cultivated to this day. Vienna has long been a seat of vibrant literary and artistic creativity: theatrical director Max Reinhardt, dramatist Arthur Schnitzler, poet Rainer Maria Rilke, modernist architect Adolf Loos, and painters Gustav Klimt and Egon Schiele are just some of Austria's world-renowned prodigies. The philosopher of language Ludwig Wittgenstein made a profound contribution to the history of ideas, while turn-of-the-20th-century Vienna was home to psychiatrist Sigmund Freud, whose theories about the nature of the unconscious have had incalculable influence on the modern understanding of human behavior.

Above all it is in music that Austria has left its greatest mark on international culture. Austria has a musical tradition that extends back to the Middle Ages, although it did not really become distinctive from the German mainstream until the 17th century. Three sources in particular encouraged the growth of a unique Austrian style: the country's monastic orders, which were reinvigorated in the 1700s by the Jesuit priesthood; court composers attracted to the new riches of the Habsburgs and their princes; and popular theater in the towns and cities, such as the Viennese Singspiel. All these combined to create a revolution in form and taste that saw Vienna dominate the world of music throughout the late 18th and 19th centuries, when it arguably became the Western world's cultural capital.

Vienna's composers have been both imports from elsewhere in Europe, like Ludwig van Beethoven, Johannes Brahms, and

Franz Lehar (composer of the popular operetta *The Merry Widow*) as well as home-grown talents such as Franz Joseph Haydn, Franz Schubert, the Strauss family—father Johann and his sons Johann Baptist and Josef—and Gustav Mahler. One figure stands out in particular, however—Austria's most towering creative genius, Wolfgang Amadeus Mozart (1756–1791).

Mozart was born in the bishopric of Salzburg, and his precocious youth has become the stuff of legend: At three years old he could pick out tunes on the harpsichord, at five he composed a concerto, and at six he performed for Empress Maria Theresa at the imperial court. Before he reached his teenage years, Mozart was conducting international tours of Europe's great capitals and writing prodigious quantities of highly original music. After serving a decade at the Salzburg court, he moved to Vienna in 1781, where he worked independently of royal patronage to produce many of his most enduring works, including the classic operas *The Abduction from the Seraglio* and *Don Giovanni* and the more comic *Cosi Fan Tutte, The Marriage of Figaro,* and *The Magic Flute.* In all, Mozart produced 41 orchestral symphonies, 23 piano sonatas, and a huge number of pieces for small chamber ensembles. He remains one of the world's unmatched geniuses, with a peerless ability to write melodies of great beauty set to masterful musical forms. His final years are still the subject of controversy among music historians, but he seems to have plunged heavily into debt and was buried in a common, unmarked, and as yet unidentified grave. Since his death, however, Austria has never forgotten Wolfgang Amadeus, and his image dominates the country's tourist-oriented literature, especially that of Salzburg.

Since 1945 Vienna has often been viewed as a conservative center of musical culture, more concerned with preserving its "heritage" than with developments going on elsewhere in Europe and the United States. Orchestras like the Vienna

Philharmonic—which until quite recently had no women musicians—developed a reputation for solid but hidebound performance, good for hearing expensive Mozart renditions but much less innovative and exciting than those in cities elsewhere in the world that were less weighed down by their historical tradition. Happily, since the 1980s there has been a revival of the Viennese musical scene, and the work being performed there is much more original and imaginative. The musical tradition in Austria also lives on through such long-running institutions as the Salzburg Festival and the Hofburg Chapel's world-famous Vienna Boys' Choir. Many musicians continue to come to Austria's capital to imbibe the rich artistic tradition and to learn from the city's musical legends.

As Austria faces the social, environmental, and economic challenges of the future, she strives to preserve and honor her past, as symbolized by this small mountain chapel overlooking the Ötztal Valley.

8

The Future of Austria

Austrians have faced two key problems in their history. The first is geographical: how to successfully settle and exploit the beautiful but austere and forbidding land that they inhabit. The second is psychological: deciding whom the Austrians are and what their nation should be about. We have discussed Austria's past and present throughout this book. Now perhaps we should speculate a little more on the country's future.

So far as their land is concerned, Austrians of the 21st century face the challenge of maintaining their foothold on a fragile and easily tarnished landscape. As we have seen, the material progress that Austria has enjoyed in the last 100 years has not been without environmental cost. The Alpine mountains, dense forests, and deep waters of the Danube have all suffered significant ecological damage as the effects of industrialization and the modern age's advances in transport and communication have taken their toll. For all of their collective wealth, modern Austrians rely on a relatively small and precious amount of sustainable land and water that they cannot afford to see spoiled. They will have to harness their native ingenuity to the task of securing economic growth and prosperity while protecting the natural environment on which they depend. And they must work in partnership alongside those neighboring countries with which they share these finite resources.

The identity dilemma is another enduring challenge. The success of the democratic Austrian Federal Republic in the second half of the 20th century has created among its people a genuine sense of national self-consciousness; very few Austrians today would see the old dream of Anschluss with another German-speaking state as a viable or meaningful option. However, there is a danger that pride in the unique Austrian achievement could ossify into a sullen, insular attitude toward the world. Austrians are already wrestling with the very real question of European integration as well as the tension between the older indigenous community and those new Austrians who have settled in the country since World War II. How will Austria's economic structure adapt to globalization, which it is in some ways ill prepared to handle? Can the Austrian state maintain its commitment to a comprehensive social security system with rising costs and a troubling national debt?

There are no simple solutions to any of these problems. However, Austrians would do well to remember that their society has traditionally flourished when it is at its most cosmopolitan, welcoming, and curious. Mozart, Wittgenstein, and Freud all had a vigorous intellectual relationship with the world beyond Austria's borders, and many of the talents who so enriched Austria's culture were originally foreigners to its soil.

Facts at a Glance

Land and People

Official Name Republic of Austria (Republik Österreich).

Capital and Seat of Government Vienna (1991 population: 1,533,000).

Other Major Cities Graz (1991 population 232,000), Linz (202,000), Salzburg (143,000), Innsbruck (114,000).

Language German.

Area 32,378 square miles (83,858 square kilometers).

Population 8.07 million (1998 census).

Population Density 249 persons per square mile (1998 census).

Religion 78 percent Roman Catholic, 5 percent Protestant, 17 percent none or other.

Highest Point Grossglockner, 12,460 feet (3,798 meters).

Mountain Ranges Austrian Alps (Bavarian, Carnic, Kitzbühel, Lechtal, Ötzal Ranges).

Major Rivers Danube, Drava, Enns, Inn, Mur.

Economy

Currency Euro (replaced Austrian schilling in January 2002).

Chief Agricultural Products Grain, fruits, potatoes, sugar beets.

Major Industries Construction, machinery, vehicles and parts, food, chemicals, lumber and wood processing, paper and paperboard, communications equipment, tourism.

Natural Resources Iron ore, oil, timber, magnesite, lead, coal, lignite, copper, hydropower.

Government

Form Federal Republic.

Suffrage 19 years of age, universal. Compulsory for presidential elections.

Legislative Assembly Bicameral: two legislative houses, National Council (Nationalrat), Federal Council (Bundesrat).

Head of Government Chancellor.

Head of State President.

Political Divisions Nine self-governing *Länder* (provinces): Burgenland, Carinthia, Lower Austria, Upper Austria, Salzburg, Styria, Tyrol, Vienna, and Vorarlberg.

History at a Glance

7000 B.C.	Earliest known human settlement of Austria.
1000–400 B.C.	Halstatt civilization.
400–15 B.C.	Celtic civilization (kingdom of Noricum).
15 B.C.–405 A.D.	Roman occupation.
782	Franks establish Eastern March.
880	Magyars conquer Eastern March.
955	Eastern March re-established by Frankish King Otto I.
976	Leopold of Babenberg made Margrave of Eastern March. Beginning of Babenberg period.
1246	Death of the last Babenberg, Duke Frederick II.
1273	Rudolf of Habsburg elected Holy Roman Emperor.
1278	Rudolf conquers Otaker II of Bohemia at the Battle of the Marchfeld and becomes Duke of Austria. Beginning of Habsburg period.
1365	University of Vienna founded.
1440	Frederick III elected Holy Roman Emperor. Habsburgs continue to hold the title almost without interruption until the empire's dissolution in 1806.
1516	Charles V becomes king of Spain, completing his enormous territorial inheritance.
1521	Charles hands over power in Austria to his brother Ferdinand. Division of the Habsburg family into Austrian and Spanish houses.
1526	King Louis of Bohemia and Hungary killed by Ottoman Turks at the Battle of Mohács. Ferdinand claims both titles but is able to gain complete control only of Bohemia.
1529	Ottomans unsuccessfully besiege Vienna.
1618–1648	Thirty Years' War.
1683	Ottomans attempt second unsuccessful siege of Vienna. In the ensuing rout, Austria conquers all of Hungary.
1701–1714	War of the Spanish Succession.
1716–1750	Main years of Baroque artistic period.
1740–1748	War of the Austrian Succession.
1756–1763	Seven Years' War.
1781–1791	Wolfgang Amadeus Mozart composing in Vienna.
1792–1815	French Revolutionary and Napoleonic Wars. Abolition of Holy Roman Empire (1806). Period ends with Congress of Vienna.

1815–1848	Main years of Biedermeier artistic period.
1848–1849	Revolution throughout Austrian Empire. Hungarian uprising quelled by Russian troops. Franz-Josef becomes emperor.
1848–1897	Main years of Historicist artistic period.
1866	Austro-Prussian War.
1867	"Compromise" (Ausgleich) with Hungary: Empire renamed Austria-Hungary.
1897–1918	Main years of Jugendstil artistic period.
1914–1918	World War I, precipitated by the assassination of Archduke Franz Ferdinand in Sarajevo (1914).
1916	Death of Emperor Franz-Josef.
1918	World War I ends with collapse of Austro-Hungarian Empire. End of the Habsburg period.
1919	Treaty of St. Germain. Federal Republic of Austria created.
1927	"Black Friday" police action against left-wing demonstrators leaves over 90 dead.
1931	Collapse of the Creditanstalt bank ushers in the Great Depression.
1933–1934	Political crisis. Chancellor Dollfuss suspends parliament, suppresses Social Democrat uprising, is killed in unsuccessful Nazi putsch.
1938	Anschluss (union) between Austria and Nazi Germany.
1939–1945	World War II. Ends with Austria occupied by France, Great Britain, United States, and USSR.
1955	Austrian State Treaty. Second Federal Republic created.
1966	End of Grand Coalition between socialists and People's Party.
1986	Kurt Waldheim elected president under great controversy.
1995	Austria joins European Union (EU).
1999	Right-wing Freedom Party of Austria joins government. Diplomatic sanctions imposed by EU.
2002	Austria replaces its own currency, the schilling, with the EU euro.

Glossary

Anschluss: The unification of Austria with Nazi Germany in March 1938, which brought the country under the leadership of Adolf Hitler until Germany's defeat at the end of World War II.

Austrian People's Party (ÖVP): The successor to the Christian Social Party, a right-of-center political movement that, along with the Social Democrats, has governed Austria throughout most of the postwar period.

Austrian State Treaty: The 1955 agreement that returned postwar Austria to the status of an independent country. Among other provisions, the treaty demanded that Austria remain politically neutral during the Cold War.

Babenbergs: The first of Austria's long-ruling dynasties, which controlled the country from 976 to 1246.

Freedom Party of Austria (FPÖ): The controversial extreme-right political party that joined the Austrian coalition government in the 1980s and 1990s.

Habsburg: The dynasty that ruled Austria from 1278 until the dissolution of its empire in 1918.

Holy Roman Empire: A loose confederation of hundreds of small, mostly German states, which was founded in 800 A.D. by Charlemagne and ruled almost without interruption from Vienna from the 15th century until its disbandment in 1806.

Proporz: A system of "proportionality" in which the major Austrian political parties assign government positions according to their relative electoral strength. A compromise agreement said to characterize the atmosphere of the post-1945 Austrian state.

St. Germain, Treaty of: One of the many peace treaties signed in 1919 ending World War I, which broke up the old Habsburg Empire into several nation-states, including the Federal Republic of Austria.

Social Democratic Party (SPÖ): One of Austria's major political parties, originally Marxist but now moderately left wing.

Further Reading

The Library of Congress has published an excellent introduction to Austria as part of its *Country Survey* series, available both in print (Washington: U.S. Government Printing Office, 1994) and on the World Wide Web (*lcweb2.loc.gov/frd/cs/attoc.html*). Other useful websites full of information include the Austria Café (*www.austria-cafe.com/*) and the Republic of Austria's own English-language homepage (*www.austria.gv.at/e/oesterreich/index.htm*). The best general history of Austria in print is probably Gordon Brook-Shepherd's *The Austrians: A Thousand-Year Odyssey* (New York: Carroll and Graf, 1996). An interesting book on one of Austria's most important rulers is Alan Warwick Palmer's *Twilight of the Habsburgs: The Life and Times of Emperor Franz Josef* (New York: Grove Press, 1995), while *What Life Was Like: At Empire's End: Austro-Hungarian Empire 1848–1918* (New York: Time-Life Books, 2000) is a good introduction to the period for younger readers. William M. Johnston's *The Austrian Mind: An Intellectual and Social History 1848–1938* (Berkeley: University of California Press, 1983) provides a useful background to the work of Sigmund Freud and other turn-of-the-20th-century Austrian thinkers. *Wittgenstein's Vienna* by Allan Janik and Stephen Toulmin (Chicago: Ivan R. Dee, 1996) is a challenging read, but it, too, reveals much about the intellectual milieu of the great philosopher. *Mozart: A Life* by Maynard Solomon (New York: HarperCollins, 1996) is a recent and highly praised biography of Austria's most famous musical son. Rolf Toman, Gerald Zugmann, and Achim Bednorz's *Vienna: Art and Architecture* (Köhl: Könemann, 1999) is a large and well-illustrated survey of one of the most beautiful cities in Europe. Those lucky enough to be visiting Austria will find both Susan Roraff and Julie Krejci's *Culture Shock! Austria* (Portland, Ore.: Graphic Arts Center, 2001) and Jonathan Bousfield and Rob Humphreys' *The Rough Guide to Austria* (London: Rough Guides, 2001) indispensable. Finally, no reading list about Austria would be complete without *The Sound of Music: The Making of America's Favorite Movie* by Julia Antopol Hirsch and Robert Wise (New York: McGraw Hill, 1993), which includes information about the real-life von Trapp family. Maria von Trapp tells *The Story of the Trapp Family Singers* in her own words, too (New York: HarperCollins, 2002).

Bibliography

Bousfield, Jonathan, and Rob Humphreys. *The Rough Guide to Austria* (London: Rough Guides, 2001).

Brook-Shepherd, Gordon. *The Austrians: A Thousand-Year Odyssey* (New York: Carroll and Graf, 1996).

Encyclopedia Britannica (www.britannica.com/).

Fichtner, Paula. *Historical Dictionary of Austria* (Lanham, Md.: Scarecrow Press, 1999).

Johnson, Lonnie. *Introducing Austria: A Short History* (Riverside, Calif.: Ariadne Press, 1989).

Riemer, Andrew. *The Habsburg Café* (Angus and Robertson, 1993).

Roraff, Susan, and Julie Krejci. *Culture Shock! Austria* (Portland, Ore.: Graphic Arts Center, 2001).

Sandford, John, editor. *Encylopedia of Contemporary German Culture* (New York: Routledge, 1999).

Solsten, Eric, and David McClave. *Austria: A Country Study* (Washington: U.S. Government Printing Office, 1994). See also *lcweb2.loc.gov/frd/cs/attoc.html*.

Statistics from the *2001 New York Times Almanac* (New York: Penguin, 2001), the *CIA World Factbook 2001* (*www.cia.gov/cia/publications/factbook/*) and the *Encyclopedia Britannica* (www.britannica.com/).

Index

Index

Picture Credits

page:

8: © Adam Woolfitt/Corbis
10: Associated Press, AP
11: © Michael Maslan Historic Photographs/ Corbis
14: © Eye Ubiquitous/Corbis
19: © Adam Woolfitt/Corbis
24: © Adam Woolfitt/Corbis
30: Archivo Iconografico, S.A./Corbis
34: © Historical Picture Archive/Corbis
37: Archivo Iconografico, S.A./Corbis
41: © Bettmann/Corbis
48: © José F. Poblete/Corbis

55: © Corbis
56: © Corbis
60: © Dallas and John Heaton/Corbis
68: © Hulton-Deutsch Collection/Corbis
72: Associated Press, AP
74: © José F. Poblete/Corbis
79: © Owen Franken/Corbis
80: © Tim Thompson/Corbis
84: © Jim Zuckerman/Corbis
87: © Otto Lang/Corbis
90: © Austrian Archive/Corbis
96: © Roman Soumar/Corbis

Cover: © Adam Woolfitt/Corbis

Frontis: Flag courtesy of theodora.com/flags. Used with permission.

About the Author

ALAN ALLPORT was born in Whiston, England, grew up in East Yorkshire, and now lives in Philadelphia. A Ph.D. candidate in the Department of History at the University of Pennsylvania, with a special interest in 19th and 20th century European history, he is currently working on projects connected to the social and cultural histories of the two world wars. The author would like to thank Tom Deveson, whose family heritage in, intimate knowledge of, and love for Austria have been invaluable in the writing of this book.